30

30

REFLECTIONS OF RESILIENCE, GROWTH, AND AN AGE NO LONGER FEARED

BRIANNA LEE DIPIETRO

NEW DEGREE PRESS

COPYRIGHT © 2021 BRIANNA LEE DIPIETRO

30

Reflections of resilience, growth, and an age no longer feared

ISBN   978-1-63676-471-9   *Paperback*

          978-1-63676-472-6   *Kindle Ebook*

          978-1-63676-473-3   *Ebook*

Robert "Bob" DiPietro

March 29, 1967–June 17, 1997

Your memory and my fire, they could save a life.

Thanks for the match.
Love endlessly,
Little Bit.

CONTENTS

———

INTRODUCTION   9

1. MAKE GOOD   15
2. THE LIFE WE BUILT   23
3. FROZEN IN TIME   33
4. KEEP GOING   45
5. PERPENDICULAR PATHS   53
6. STILL   65
7. DRIPS ON A ROCK   77
8. CARING FOR OUR CHILDREN   87
9. LOVE YOU MORE   101
10. CREATING CALM   109
11. 330 DAYS   121
12. BETTER YET   137

    RESOURCES   149
    ACKNOWLEDGMENTS   155
    APPENDIX   161
    ENDNOTES   167

INTRODUCTION

———

A cold grocery store.
A black answering machine blinking red.
My pregnant mom, crying.
A teddy bear in the back of a cop car.

At 3 p.m. on June 17, 1997, Robert Joseph DiPietro was shot and killed outside of the Roadhouse Pub in Peabody, Massachusetts.

He was thirty. I was six.

I kept my mouth shut and my mind heavy for the next fifteen years, too scared to ask my family anything about that day for fear of tipping the scale on their mental and emotional load.

In elementary and middle school, I even told my friends an elaborate story about how my dad died a hero.

"A man came to his work with a gun, wanting to shoot someone else," I'd say. "But then *my* dad stepped in front of the gun just as it went off, and he saved someone's life."

I'd come to find out this wasn't true, but I didn't know that then, and I wanted to give him the story he deserved.

Drowning in questions and grief, I thought it better not to use my story as a buoy.

I dipped in and out of therapy, ate and purged my feelings, and cried myself to sleep when no one could hear me.

I imagined every way he could have been shot and played each scenario on repeat in my mind; so much so I felt physically ill anytime a gun went off on TV or a car backfired nearby.

Finally, old enough to be allowed on the internet, I didn't just play games or chat endlessly via instant messenger like other kids were doing at my age. Instead, I searched and searched for answers regarding my dad's death in secrecy, but nothing was there to find.

With dial-up internet and one shared family computer, I had limited time to research. I would also come to find out that all news coverage of his death was in print. It left no mark in the early digital world.

In June 2013, I got my first big girl job in public relations. I was introduced to an online resource that monitors for print media coverage as part of my training. This tool, I quickly realized, allowed me to search for anything that was ever printed in a newspaper.

This is it, I thought. *My way out.*

I would find newspaper clippings from the day he died, and maybe even articles on the court proceedings that followed. I would get answers to all my questions, and I would set myself free from the weight of grief I had carried for more than a decade.

Sitting in my high-walled, gray polyester cubicle, peeking over my shoulder every so often to make sure my new coworkers weren't eyeing the non-work research I was conducting, I typed my dad's name, plus some unfortunate keywords—"gun," "shot," and "killed"—and set the date range for June 1997.

After all that time, there it was.

The Boston Globe, "Attempt at Peace Proved Fatal," by Paul Langner, Staff Writer, June 19, 1997

> *The shooting of an Essex man in broad daylight, allegedly by his friend and business partner, was brought on by the victim's attempt to calm his friend down.*
>
> *Jerry Richard McIntire killed Robert DiPietro with one shot to the chest and immediately regretting it, knelt over the dying man and pleaded with him not to die.*

On that dreaded day, inside the pub, McIntire claimed that "there were people out to get him" and that he needed to "get it over with."

My dad then followed McIntire out to his truck, and minutes later, my dad was dead. No one will ever know what ensued in that parking lot.

So, instead of answers, all I got that day were more questions.

I don't remember it like it was yesterday—maybe because I was six or maybe because that's what your brain does when it's trying to protect you. It shields bad memories behind a thick, pain-free illusion of a wall. But as years go by, it seems, that wall is crumbling down, and scattered flashes of details are coming into view.

A cold grocery store. A black answering machine blinking red. My pregnant mom, crying. A teddy bear in the back of a cop car. A bright, white room with no windows. And my sister screaming, "NO!"

Now I can name these memories, this experience, and others in my life as trauma.

The Center for the Treatment of Anxiety and Mood Disorders says trauma is a psychological, emotional response to an event or an experience deeply distressing or disturbing (Center for the Treatment of Anxiety and Mood Disorders, 2021).

And according to the American Psychological Association, long-term reactions (may) include unpredictable emotions, flashbacks, strained relationships, and even physical symptoms (American Psychological Association, 2021).

To me, trauma is completely personal—personal in that if you experience something that feels traumatic to you, no matter the circumstance, it's yours to call trauma.

My family and I are not alone in our trauma as victims of gun violence. Every day, over one hundred Americans are killed with guns, and two hundred more are shot and wounded. These numbers don't account for loved ones who also suffer as a result (Everytown for Gun Safety Support Fund, 2021).

Ours is just one type of trauma. Seventy percent of US adults have experienced some type of traumatic event at least once in their lives.

That's more than 220 million people in this country alone.

As a kid, my mom helped care for her drug-addicted brother, long before losing her husband to gun violence. My partner's mother was diagnosed with breast cancer, twice. And have I mentioned my divorce? That happened young—with a brand-new baby—and it almost did me in.

All, in their own right, *traumatic.*

We are not broken.

That is what this book is about.

Not my dad's life and death, though I'd love to write that prequel. It's about stories of post-traumatic growth, and the extreme potential I've found within humans who have gone through shit—including myself.

Though cliché, I do believe that what doesn't kill us makes us stronger. Because for me, learning to *grow*—and not just *go*—through trauma has changed my life.

I believe that traumatic experiences have made me who I am. I know I am much more empathetic and understanding, both to myself and to those around me, because of what I've been through. I also know the fire I feel within me was born from harm but fuels me to do some good.

Maybe in sharing these experiences with you—of loss, tragedy, missteps, fear, and even better yet, growth—you'll find resonance (and, a girl can dream, inspiration). Maybe it will show you the domino effects of trauma and how I and some beautiful humans I know have learned to rebuild. Maybe, it will simply offer some comfort as you navigate experiences all your own.

And, if you've been moved deeply by the need to end gun violence in America, you'll learn about some of the best and most immediate ways you can get involved.

*My dad with my sister Amanda (center) and me (right) in Errol,
NH in 1991. Photo credit: Shelley Mullarkey (Mom)*

1

MAKE GOOD

———

I don't remember if this is the exact order
in which she said these words,
but I do remember the weight of them.
How they sucked the air out of that very small, all-white,
fluorescent-lit room.

You know that sharp, sudden pain you feel when you push the Q-Tip a little *too* far into your ear? There you are just going about your daily routine and then *JAB*. You've done exactly what the box says not to do. You wince and close your eyes tight, wondering when the agony will subside.

That's what it feels like every time I think about my dad's death.

It's also how I felt the first time I read Jerry McIntire's obituary.

I always thought I'd confront my dad's murderer. Look him in the eye, make sure that he was, at a minimum, less happy than me.

I was ready for this, after years of wondering.

But, before I could do so, he died.

A murderer is supposed to die alone, in jail, with only remorse to hold onto. But, in late November 2012, my mom got word that my dad's murderer was dead. He was not alone, nor in jail. According to his obituary, he was "a loving uncle, and dear stepfather."

On October 1, 1997, 106 days after he senselessly shot and killed my dad outside of some hole-in-the-wall pub, Jerry McIntire pleaded not guilty in Salem District Court. One swing of the gavel, a short sentence, and an early release for good behavior, and McIntire was free. Before his own thirtieth birthday, he put my dad's death behind him and started anew.

Something I would never be able to do.

My mom once met McIntire in jail. "It was an accident," he told her. "Bob was such a great guy. We were friends. I would never have wanted to hurt him!"

She looked on, shattered with grief, but with her chin held high.

"Bob wouldn't want me to hate you," she said. "He wouldn't want me to walk through the rest of my life with that hate in my heart. So, I won't."

He told her he had pictures of me and my siblings in his jail cell, so he had to wake up to see our faces every day to remind him of the pain he caused.

"Someday, when I'm out of here, I promise you I will work to help spread the word about accidental shootings. I will speak at schools…I will do something to make amends," he said.

My mom, who knows the tolls of trauma all too well, also knows how easily it can go awry and how hard post-traumatic growth can be for some people.

McIntire never made good on his promise to her. For years after his release, she received messages from the victims' advocate notifying her that he was back in jail.

"I have no clue why, and I never wanted to know. I can only assume it was because of drugs and other demons," she told me. "I couldn't waste any more of my energy on a person who was a lost and hopeless cause."

Guided by her outlook and strength, I too learned to find peace in his sentence and passing. Not because he's gone, but because while he lived, he floundered. He suffered from the same demons that helped him shoot my dad that day and the new ones that found him after he realized what he did.

A letter from Jerry McIntire to me and my siblings on July 11, 1999, a month before he was released on early parole:

You don't know who I am. My name is Jerry McIntire. I am the person responsible for your father's death. I am so truly sorry from the bottom of my heart. I know I could not say I am sorry enough. I would do anything to go back in time and change that day. I wish I was not writing this letter to you three today. I never meant to hurt your dad ... I was careless and irresponsible with the handling of a gun. It was a terrible accident ... he did not deserve to be taken away from the three of you and your mother, as you don't deserve to go through this either. When I am released from prison someday, I am going to speak to kids and adults about the dangers of guns. They are so dangerous. All it takes is one second of carelessness and your whole life and many others are changed forever. I want to try and get this message across and even if I change only a few people's minds about buying a gun, it may save a life.

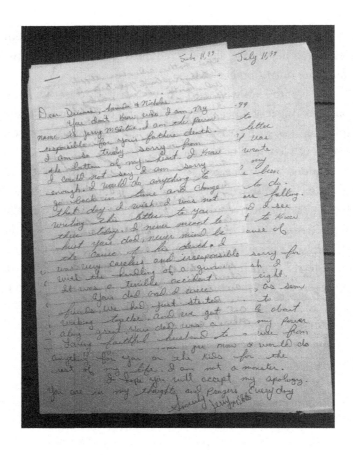

A letter from Jerry McIntire to me and my siblings from his jail cell on July 11, 1999.

Tuesday, June 17, 1997 started out like any other day.

My dad was up and out before the dawn, headed for work at DiPietro Logging and Land Clearing—his very own business and one he was finally getting off the ground.

Mom rushed around, seven months pregnant, making breakfast and lunches for my nine-year-old sister Amanda and six-year-old me.

We lived approximately fifty steps from Essex Elementary School where Amanda was finishing third grade, I was closing out kindergarten, and Mom worked as an administrative assistant in special education.

After school that day, the three of us hopped in the car and drove twenty minutes to the nearest grocery store. Right around 3 p.m., as Dad was shot in the chest a mere eight miles away, we were deciding between chicken patties or Hamburger Helper for dinner.

In the serenity of a cold produce aisle, we couldn't be reached.

It was the nineties. Cellphones weren't as commonplace, so Mom would go straight from work to the grocery store without a phone because she didn't have one. And we would assume that, per usual, we would arrive home to see Daddy in his dirty work clothes, with his feet up on the table, coffee cup in hand.

But that's not how it would go. We went an hour, together, not knowing everything had changed for good.

We left the grocery store and drove twenty minutes back to our apartment. Mom was seven months pregnant and very tired. "Where is your father? I thought he'd be here to help," she muttered. "He must still be at work. Girls, grab as many bags as you can. Let's try to do this in one trip."

We walked through the front door and down one flight of stairs to our home. She fumbled with her keys.

Once inside, we dropped our bags in the kitchen to the left, and Mom went straight for the answering machine blinking red in the living room to the right. She hit "Play."

"Shell…," said my grandfather Carl. His voice was low, slow, and somber. "It's Dad…you need to call right away. Bob's had an accident and was taken to Salem Hospital."

My mom picked up the landline and dialed his number. "What happened?" she asked.

"An Essex police officer will be there shortly to pick you up. He'll take you to the hospital. Please accept a ride from him. We'll see you soon," he said. She hung up the phone.

"We have to go," she said, rushing us back out the door.

My sister grabbed her teddy bear, and we walked upstairs and out the front door just as a cop car was pulling up with its lights on. A police officer stepped out of his vehicle and opened its rear doors.

"Is he dead?" she asked him, point blank.

He looked at her, didn't say a word, and waved us in.

The three of us cried the whole thirty-minute ride to Salem, though we weren't sure why. And, besides pulling up under a big red "EMERGENCY" sign, the rest of that evening is a blur.

Mom was taken away from us in a hurry, and Amanda, her teddy bear, and I were seated in a waiting room with family and friends. No one said a word, but everyone was crying.

When Mom entered the room, she was wheeled in by a nurse with a wheelchair. And the three of us—Mom, Amanda, and I—were whisked away into a private room.

"Daddy's dead. He's not coming back. You're not going to see him anymore," said Mom.

I don't remember if this is the exact order in which she said these words, but I do remember the weight of them. How they sucked the air out of that very small, all-white, fluorescent-lit room.

Did he see me before he left for work? Did he tell me he loved me? What did he listen to on his way to work? Was his last meal any good?

Was he happy?

It has now been twenty-four years since Dad died, yet these questions still bubble to the surface, ever so slowly, and then, as if my insides reach a boiling point, all at once.

His death haunts me, but it's also a part of me. I don't think I'll ever shake the trauma of it all, but I'm coming to learn that I don't think I ever want to.

With every bit of pain, comes one fierier bit of passion.

Passion to educate myself on gun sense issues in this country. Passion to share my story and inspire others to do the same. And passion to step in and make good on Jerry McIntire's promise to my mother because he never could.

2

THE LIFE WE BUILT

———

Now on the floor, she grabbed on,
holding us together as tight as she could.

My mom, Shelley, found out she was pregnant with my sister when she was seventeen years old.

In shock, she was too scared to tell her parents right away, and she wasn't ready to tell the baby's father, her boyfriend at the time.

"We were barely hanging on as it was," she said. "Before I ever told him I was pregnant, it was the beginning of the end. He didn't want to be a part of our relationship anymore, and I worried he wouldn't want any part of having a child either," she told me.

But Bob, she thought. She could trust Bob. He would know what to do.

Mom met Bob in 1984 at the Essex Agricultural Technical Institute.

"Looking back, I think it was fate," she said. "We were both kind of confused, and a little lost in school. I didn't want to face the pressures of public high school and was looking for an easy way out. He had trouble in his public school and was trying to make it in a place where he could nurture his taste for the outdoors."

Mom enrolled in animal science and horse management, not knowing she'd be slaughtering animals, milking cows, and cleaning stalls. Bob, who always loved the outdoors, excelled in ornamental horticulture and landed a job at the local garden center learning how to landscape.

She can't explain it, but they just "clicked."

Bob grew up in a stable home in a middle-class neighborhood and was used to family dinners, vacations, and religion. Mom was from, as she likes to put it, "the wrong side of the tracks," with divorced parents and a mother struggling to find an affordable home and make ends meet.

But during those unique four years of high school tending to plants and herding animals, the two of them found their own little corner of the world, and without truly realizing what was happening, they grew extremely close.

When Mom found out she was pregnant, she and Bob were just friends. Up until that point, both had other love interests, and enjoyed the revelries of high school in the '80s.

Things came to a screeching halt with the news that she would soon be a mom. At the time, Bob had a girlfriend but was always there for Shelley when she needed him.

So, she confided in Bob first, and he became her rock. Between him, her mother Paula, and most importantly, herself, she came to find out she had just what she needed to step into this unexpected chapter of her life.

Mom graduated in 1987 by the skin of her teeth and finished high school just in time to give birth to my sister Amanda in December. Mom and Amanda then lived with Paula while she worked to be able to support the two of them on her own.

Her relationship with Bob grew into a romantic one, and though Amanda's teenage biological father tried to be involved at first, he ultimately decided to sign his rights over to Bob so he could adopt her.

Not long after, on February 24, 1991, Mom and Bob got married in front of seventy-five people at the Knights of Columbus in Swampscott, Massachusetts.

"At the wedding, I was six months pregnant with you!" she told me. The wedding was planned for September of that year, but the surprise news of my pending arrival pushed the wedding into the cold of winter.

"It wasn't the fairytale wedding, but it was very meaningful," she said. "For the first time in my life, I felt whole, safe, and secure."

Over the next six years, their lives together took them to Errol, New Hampshire, where Bob could be one with the woods and his dream of starting his own logging business would become more of a plan. They then found themselves back in Massachusetts when Shelley was craving the comfort of a familiar setting.

In Massachusetts, our family found community. Mom worked first at the same preschool my sister and I attended, and then at our elementary school. Outside of those work hours, she helped Dad get his business off the ground. And on November 8, 1993, DiPietro Land Clearing was incorporated as a joint business venture of their own in their tiny little town of Essex.

"For a long time, we believed that our family would consist of just the four of us," Mom said. "Bob and I would make the best life together for ourselves and our girls. We wouldn't have any more kids, we couldn't afford it. Instead, we would concentrate on the business and our future. Someday, we would buy a home for our girls to grow up in. Amanda could have her very own room, and Breezy, her puppy."

But in early 1996, they got the bug. Before they knew what happened, they were seriously discussing trying one more time for a boy. "Our consciences told us this probably wasn't the smartest decision we ever made, and some family members agreed, but our hearts won out. I'm so glad they did," she said.

By the end of that year, Mom was pregnant, and in early 1997, they found out they were in fact having the boy they wanted.

As Mom's belly grew, so did Dad's business. He landed long-term land clearing contracts—worth more than either of them had yet to see—and he purchased his very own piece of heavy machinery. His beloved skidder.

As a family, we celebrated Dad's thirtieth birthday, Mom's twenty-seventh, and my sixth. We even snuck in Mother's Day and our very last Father's Day.

On June 17, 1997, Mom was seven months pregnant with Nick, the boy they didn't know they needed, until they just did.

By the end of her workday, she was exhausted. She knew she had to go grocery shopping or they wouldn't have anything for dinner, nor breakfast the following day. So, she rushed to get us girls out of school, in the car, and to the store.

When we returned from grocery shopping, Dad's truck was nowhere to be seen. Mom was pregnant and pissed. He was late from work, which would mean she wouldn't have any help with the bags and she'd have to start dinner alone.

"As soon as we got into our apartment, I noticed the answering machine blinking away," she said.

She hit play and was struck by the desperation in her father's tone. "I could hear the seriousness in his voice before he even said the words "Shell...it's Dad. You need to call right away. Bob's had an accident."

"I couldn't breathe. My heart was pounding. My pregnant stomach was cramping with pain. The grocery bags were scattered around the room," she recalled.

She grabbed us girls and took us outside where a police car was waiting. The Essex Chief of Police stepped out of his vehicle.

"Is he dead?" she cried.

He did not answer, but she saw the tears in his eyes. She collapsed in his arms and fell to the ground. He pulled her back up and got all of us into the car.

On the way to the hospital in the back of a cop car, we could not stop crying. "I was crying, but I still didn't know why. Both of you were crying because I was upset. And I couldn't stop myself from asking the chief, 'Car accident? Chainsaw? Work accident?'" she said.

He wouldn't answer her.

"We entered the first set of doors only to be whisked away from the police officer by two people dressed in scrubs," she said.

We walked down a long hospital corridor to find, to her surprise, my dad's brother, her brother-in-law, also in scrubs. He happened to work at this ER and was on duty on this very day. Crying, he reached out to hold her.

"Shell, he's gone," he said, just to her.

Family came pouring out into the hall and took us girls into a waiting area. A surgeon took my mom to a chair nearby.

"Bob has passed away. I'm so sorry, Mrs. DiPietro. We did everything we could to save him," he said.

Mom can't recall what was said after that. She was in shock. "I couldn't speak. I couldn't even cry anymore. It took me an hour or so to realize they had actually told me he was shot," she said.

The rest was a flurry. She was shuffled from that surgeon to the police, and then to Dad.

"My heart and mind tried to shut down. It was all too much," she said. They wheeled her in to see him, not remembering when or how she ended up in a wheelchair. Someone slowly pulled down the sheet covering his body, just enough to expose his face. She jumped up to hug and kiss him but was stopped by someone's hand.

"I'm sorry. He has a large incision in his chest from the emergency surgery. I don't want you to have to see that," they said.

"He was so cold," she said. "But he looked like he was sleeping. I kissed his forehead, and then tried to wipe the dirt off his face from work, as I'd always do. I don't know why that mattered to me at the time…but I did my duty, and I was wheeled back out. I had to leave him there."

That really bothered her, but she had another job she had to do. She had to tell her children their father was dead. "This was by far the hardest thing I've ever had to do."

Mom was wheeled from her dead husband's room back into a waiting room full of sad family and friends. But she had tunnel vision.

There, her two daughters sat, upset, and confused—both emotions worsened by the look of their mother entering the room. The nurse escorted Mom and us two children into a small, white room adjacent to the waiting area. We were shut in, alone.

Now on the floor, she grabbed on, holding us together as tight as she could. Then, she said it.

"Daddy's…dead. I'm so sorry. I'm so sorry."

"NOOOO, DADDY, NOOOO!" she remembers Amanda screaming. Together, we let out gut wrenching wails. It's the last memory she has of that day.

Trying to work, take care of the house, deal with legal proceedings, pay her bills, get her children onto a path of healing, counseling, and some kind of stability—for Mom, it all happened in a fog.

"I was just going through the motions for two full years. I don't remember anything during that time. It's super unfair to my children, and especially my newborn son. He was loved, and he was cared for…that's all I could muster."

During those first few years without Dad, she was always sad, but she did what she had to do to grow through it.

She made sure Amanda and I were in therapy and finding our way at school. She made sure she had the counseling she needed and welcomed the outpouring of help and support of her family, friends, and neighbors.

She even got up the nerve to visit the man who killed her husband. "I needed to move that pain to another place, and out of my heart. Not so close to the surface every single day. I needed to move on with my life to help me and my kids move on with ours," she said.

"But it was witnessing you kids grow, and move forward, and do your own things…that's what made me able to stand up again. I devoted my life to ensuring my children would be okay, and it helped me heal. I had purpose, and I decided to live on in Bob's memory and in honor of the life we built together," she said.

A few years later, her best friend Robyn encouraged her, quite repeatedly, to consider dating again.

"Shell, don't be mad at me, but I have someone I want you to meet," she said.

"I shut her down immediately," said Mom. "I didn't want any part of it, but I eventually agreed to let him get my number. We sat on the phone and emailed. We chatted via instant messenger for hours and hours after the kids went to bed. That's how we got to know each other."

Mom knew there was an attraction and a connection, but with everything going on, she had some concerns.

"He had been married and divorced twice already. He had three children of his own. Would he be able to give my children the attention they deserved?" she wondered.

She decided it would be easiest to be forthcoming with him from the start. "If my kids don't like you, you're out of here," she told him. "They will make this decision for all of us." She knew the 'liking' part would take some time, so she gave him the space to earn our trust.

"Do you like magic?" he asked me and my siblings on the very first night he hung out with us at our house. I was skeptical, to say the least.

I didn't want to like him. He wasn't Dad.

He waved his hands around in front of my face and pulled out a long green handkerchief from his right hand, which definitely was not there before. I did my best not to laugh or to ask how he did it.

"...Cool," I said, trying to remain visibly disinterested.

But that dang trick, and the pizza, and the nighttime trips with his three kids to our local playground, and the interest he showed in my sports…It all did a number on me over time.

We became friends. Not right away, but slow and steady and methodical, like the sand sculpture man I like to marvel at every year at the Topsfield Fair.

"These routines, these everyday things that he did—they started to give all of us some normalcy," said Mom. "The kids let him in, and it warmed my heart to see."

"Bob has a huge piece of my heart and always will," she told him while they were dating. "Nothing and no one will ever change that. If you are willing to have the rest of what's left of my heart, I'm in."

He happily and respectfully agreed, and never looked back.

"Michael won me over with his patience for my need to keep Bob's memory alive," said Mom. "The pictures of Bob all over our house he was now moving into—he never once asked me to remove any sort of memory of him. He attended our sad cemetery visits on Father's Day and birthdays just to support us. He stood back in silence and then came forward at just the right time to hold my hand or rub my back. That sense of unconditional love and support was all I needed."

Michael Mullarkey became my stepdad when they married at the most adorable bed and breakfast in New Hampshire on October 19, 2002. I do not know where any of us would be without him today.

Mom and Michael sold our childhood home in Essex, Massachusetts in early 2020 and moved into their dream home on a lake in Brookline, New Hampshire. They drink coffee on their screened-in porch overlooking the water at sunrise. They enjoy each other's company with their toasty feet pointed at a new wood stove. And they look forward to years of grandchildren's sleepovers and family dinners at a place they've worked so hard for and most certainly earned.

Mom (center-right), holding my daughter Talia, and Michael (center-left) holding my nephew Gavin.

3

FROZEN IN TIME

———

It was never to achieve some sort of
body type or look that I envied,
but rather to satisfy a voice from the
trenches of my subconscious
that told me I was no longer perfect.

"You seem stuck," said my therapist during one of our weekly evening sessions in early 2015. The room was calm and dark. Music was playing softly in the background, and rain hit the curtainless window just behind her head.

"It seems a piece of you stood still the day your father died," she continued. "That piece of you is still six years old and yearning for his approval—for a time when both you and this strong male figure in your life balanced on perfection. No wrongs, no faults, only love and adoration."

Maybe she was right.

Memories of my dad are few and far between, but when I see him in my mind, I see only his smile and his strength.

Five foot three, tattooed, and with bulging biceps from his job as a logger, he was of similar stature to Popeye.

To me, he was Daddy. I didn't know anything about his political leanings or whether I would ultimately agree with them. I didn't know if he had any faults or if he ever made mistakes. I didn't know if we would butt heads or be best friends someday.

He made jokes and held me close.

We shared the same big, almond-shaped, deep brown eyes. He always looked dirty and roughed up from a long day with a chainsaw in the trees, but he smelled quite the opposite—of cologne or deodorant, or maybe just of my daddy's girl delusions.

At six years old, what Daddy said went. And Daddy said I was perfect.

But that's when our stories parted ways. He was taken from me a lifetime too soon, and I grew, physically and emotionally, and my beliefs and opinions evolved. I gained another twenty-four years of life experiences—happiness, challenges, pains, fears, and triumphs.

I completely lost sight of the fact that he too would have changed. Maybe not in the way he loved me, but in the way I saw him, got to know him—not just as Daddy but as a human.

Together, we'd grow, in all different directions, but side by side all the same.

I found this therapist during a panicked, late-night search when I was twenty-three years old.

Alone, in an apartment I shared with my boyfriend of three years, something set me off.

I can't remember what put the idea in my head this time around, whether it was just my reflection in the mirror, or if I got a craving for something like ice cream or leftover pizza in the fridge. But alas, much like the many other nights I spent dealing with closeted, disordered eating during the past few years, I was triggered.

So, like each time before, I binged and purged; then, I dealt with the same cyclical repercussions. Extreme guilt, self-loathing, sore throat, stomach pains, and dizziness.

I called it the bulimia hangover.

But, for some reason, this hangover was different. It hurt more than my insides and my pride. It hurt my heart and I felt bad *for* me instead of *about* me.

Finally. I stuck my fingers down my throat enough times to know I probably caused some damage somewhere down there, and I was sick of feeling so inadequate.

Though it would take years to feel "free" from bulimia with some relapses, I'm forever proud of getting myself some help and constantly reminded of that one discussion with my therapist—a conversation I, for some reason, could only really have with a stranger.

She asked me what I was looking for each time I binged and purged.

I couldn't answer. I was active and fit. I had a loving boy-friend and a close group of friends. But, at the time, any anxiety, big or small, would trigger a scan of my environment.

Am I near a bathroom? Somewhere I could do this quietly? What have I eaten recently? What could I eat to make this easier? Who's going to be looking for me if I slip away? How long can I be gone before they notice?

These thoughts, of negativity and self-hate, were on a constant loop for years but at their worst in my early twenties.

My therapist dug deep for a couple of sessions, well before any memories I have of disordered eating or thoughts. Back into my childhood, and back to my dad.

That is when she so gently placed this idea in front of me. That part of me was trapped in my childhood. "Take it or leave it," I'm pretty sure was her directive. But it was there, and it hit hard.

What she introduced to me was the possibility that each time I'd sulk away into a bathroom, or the woods, or the shower even, to rid myself of what is meant to nourish me—it was never to achieve some sort of body type or look that I envied, but rather to satisfy a voice from the trenches of my subconscious that told me I was no longer perfect.

And for whatever male figure loved me or would try to love me, *I must be perfect*, because I knew what it felt like to be perfect in my dad's eyes, and I would do anything to feel that again.

Before therapy, I didn't give any thought to why I was really doing what I was doing.

I would never have connected any subconscious, childhood feelings I had about my dad with what I was doing to my body as an adult.

Stuck with the point of view of two loved little eyes and a man frozen in time, I was on some sort of lifelong pursuit to be whatever it was I thought Daddy saw in me—him at thirty and me at six.

An impossible quest.

Whether in the form of disordered eating, or in the constant, nagging way my brain reminds me I'm not perfect, I need to be better, to do better. The issues are certainly there.

And I have long had issues stemming from the loss of my dad.

In middle school, I learned about calories. I would pack my school lunch in front of my mom to ensure she thought

I was getting whatever nutrition she thought I'd need. Then, I'd eat next to nothing for breakfast and rush out the door.

At lunch, I'd play with my food as a distraction to those around me. I'd rip my sandwich in half and then in half again. I'd eat one fourth, maybe, and would be sure to talk my way through the bell for class so I could rush to get up and toss the rest of my food in the trash. Sometimes I'd stuff it all back into my backpack.

One time, my mom saw the food in my backpack and realized I didn't eat lunch that day. After she questioned me on it and I came up with some lie, I began putting less and less in my sandwiches. She'd ask school staff if I was eating, and they'd say yes. What she didn't know was that all I was eating was bread and mustard.

Win, win.

These were things I could control. Dinner, on the other hand, was a family affair. A meal filled with comfort food, and one we always had together. I could never get away from it without clearing my plate.

As high school came into view, I got more self-conscious and hyper-aware of what I deemed flaws.

I never thought of myself as attractive or cool. But boy oh hot boy, did I want to be. I wore a lot of makeup and straightened, scrunched, or crimped my hair every single day. I had girl crushes on Lizzie McGuire and Avril Lavigne, and if I was going for the look of their impossible lovechild, I absolutely nailed it.

Wearing two-layered polo shirts, gaucho pants, and Etnies skater shoes, I walked into Manchester Essex Regional High School freshman year with two goals: make friends and, for God's sake, be cool.

I spent the previous two years in the same building, just in a different hall. For seventh and eighth grade, us Essex townies were shipped over to Manchester-By-The-Sea to get acquainted with our new peers because our town was too small to have its own high school.

I spent those two years mostly observing. Who was friends with who? Who was already considered "not cool"? Who was climbing the ranks as we entered high school? I had to find my way in.

What I saw as "cool" dictated what I decided to be a part of in high school. I doubled down on sports, I quit chorus (which I loved), and when that cute pack of boys I had been trying to get close to was into something, then I was too.

This did not work out so well for me.

I had no idea who I was or wanted to be. I didn't even know what I really liked. All I knew was what these boys liked—themselves, girls, and trouble—and that was good enough for me.

My hormones were high and self-confidence was low, so I quickly fell head over heels in love with one of these boys. Like, obsessed, major-first, real-passionate-crush, one-way-street kind of love.

For the purposes of this story, let's call him Joe.

Well, Joe was best friends with Peter, Henry, and Frank. Henry showed interest in me first, not Joe. Thrilled by the attention, fifteen-year-old me immediately put Joe on the back burner as a warm lead I would continue to befriend and showed interest in Henry back. Henry and I became boyfriend and girlfriend for maybe a couple of months, but that dwindled quickly. I then fell for Frank. I fell for Frank hard.

Something I see now that I certainly did not see then, was that I was confusing relationship-building and friendship with heart-bending, break-me-to-my-core, teenage love. I was vulnerable, awkward, and pubescent. I should have just let them be my friends. I needed friends. But I confused their safety, relationship, and new bonds for romance and fairytales; and I let those lines blur repeatedly.

So, when Joe started showing me the interest and attention I wanted for so long, texting me and chatting me late at night while I was in a relationship with Frank...I failed at being the good person I knew I was at heart.

My lack of understanding for love, for myself and others, became clear. I all but jumped at the opportunity to be unfaithful to Frank.

I spent months talking to Joe incessantly and secretly.

Whenever we'd hang out as a group, Joe offered to drive me home. In these moments, I was so overjoyed with this long-desired show of affection from Joe that I let my love for Frank slip out of sight, and therefore, out of mind.

One night while hanging out in Frank's room watching a movie, my phone started buzzing incessantly. First Peter, then Henry texted me things like, *We know what you did,* and, *If you don't tell Frank, we will.*

I don't know what you're talking about, I texted back quickly while Frank was in the bathroom. *Please stop.*

But I knew exactly what they were talking about. The rush and excitement of being adored and loved by Frank while sneaking around with and constantly talking to Joe came crashing down at my feet when his phone started to blow.

His friends didn't tell him exactly what they learned about Joe and me, but they hinted at it. They told him to ask me what I did.

That late fall night, it all came out. Honestly, up until that point, father's death aside, I had never felt so much emotion at once. Until seeing the pain I caused another human with my own recklessness and lack of empathy, I didn't realize just how much I did care for Frank and how little I valued my own self-worth.

When you think about the word "trauma," you probably think of it happening *to* you. That trauma was likely something out of your control. But, in some cases, trauma can be self-inflicted.

We—Joe and I—caused this trauma. For Frank, for our friend group, and for ourselves. We threw caution (and a whole lot of hormonal feelings) to the wind, not knowing or caring where it landed. Like a boomerang, it all came back around.

High school was never the same. This happened mid-junior year, and for the next year and a half, I walked through those halls with my head down. I learned to never make eye contact, to stay quiet, and to leave as quickly as I possibly could when that final bell rang. Because what started in high school as an upward trajectory of new friends and experiences turned on a dime, into a downward spiral of bullying and isolation.

For teenagers, love can be passionate and super intense. It was the first time either of us had felt this type of emotion for another person, and that bond, once formed, felt unbreakable.

As odd as it seems, I never felt closer to Frank than I did after everything unfolded. He, for some reason, wasn't ready to let me go. So, at seventeen years old, we decided to stay together—regardless of the fact that all of his friends hated me. Regardless of the fact that I had completely betrayed his trust.

Frank constantly asked me to prove my love for him, to prove to him he could trust me again. He watched as his friends bullied me at school and turned a blind eye. He wouldn't look at me some days until we were clear from his friends' gaze.

He struggled with not wanting to let our relationship go and wanting to stay close with his friends. He became a bystander. A silent middleman in between bullies and his girlfriend, the bullied.

I felt I deserved all of it, so on and on it went.

High school became my worst nightmare. I dreaded every day I had to walk through those doors. My bullies wouldn't just whisper about me in front of me—they'd talk very loudly and in a very purposeful way.

"Slut," one would say as I walked past their endless row of lockers.

"Cheat," another would yell, blatantly masking with a cough and a laugh.

I'd walk into a classroom, and they'd joke about the smell that followed. On multiple occasions, I returned to my locker after class to find that someone poured an entire bottle of Gatorade on all my books. When I'd have to open those stained, sticky pages during class, they happily asked me what happened.

The kicker for me was that none of this negative attention ever landed on Joe. My bullies stayed friends with him. They just hung out separately—with Frank, and then somewhere else with Joe. When they called me names, I'd even catch Joe smirking, trying to play it cool. Maybe just also trying not to lose everything the way I had.

Some people stayed my friends despite it all, but not many. It wasn't long before I believed everything everyone said. I was riddled with guilt and shame, and I felt I couldn't do anything but soak in every ounce of hate.

The day I walked off those grounds in my white cap and gown was one of the most freeing moments of my life. *I can wipe myself clean from this place*, I thought. *I'll start anew at college, and I'll be the very best person I can be.*

Things didn't change overnight. Frank and I stayed together through the first year of college, still stuck in that bond we had created through the worst of it all. We fought often. He didn't trust me, and I didn't know who I was or what to do without him.

We started growing apart and finding our own way. Late freshman year, when I finally unglued myself from the comfort of his hip, I learned how to be myself in my new environment; and pretty much just like that, I started to make friends. *Real friends.* For the first time in a long time, I showed myself kindness, and it allowed me to do the same for others.

Without enough reflection or the therapy I know I desperately needed after that breakup, I decided I was ready for a major change.

Months later, in July of 2011, I found myself on a six-month study abroad trip to Australia. There, halfway across the world, was the first time I made myself throw up.

Maybe an older version of myself would have seen this collision coming.

The longstanding body and self-confidence issues. The out-of-control feeling of being truly on my own for the first time in my life. The intense breakup. The innate desire while I was there to both do it all and once again fit in and be cool.

Combined, it led to an all-out eating disorder.

By the third month in Australia, I was fifteen pounds heavier than when I arrived—a type of fast, unexpected weight gain that I never experienced before. I was living off ninety-nine-cent spaghetti, Nutella sandwiches, and boxed wine, and one day something in my brain just flipped.

I saw a picture someone posted on Facebook of me, and my insides screamed. *Fix this. You are alone. No one loves you. You have lost control. Look at yourself. Lose the weight. Be better.*

I ran for my bathroom.

Though it was the first time I physically hurt myself, I now see and understand it was a culmination of a long-formed recipe for disaster and an unwillingness to see my need for help.

A destructive and, until this point, unreasonable desire to be perfect—one that dominoed into a complete lack of self-respect, an incapability to love others in the ways they deserved, and ultimately some super harmful and mentally debilitating form of hate.

On that evening in 2015, sitting across the room from my new, mellow-tempered, middle-aged stranger friend of a therapist, I was offered this reflection from start to finish. I don't know if it ultimately saved me, but it gave me the big picture I needed to start to move forward.

To get healthy, and to find a better outlet.

In some of the same ways losing my father to gun violence made me appreciate life and living in the now, all these experiences since his death, for better or for worse, made me that much more capable of appreciating people, relationships, and love for all they are.

Love for one another as people with feelings, traumas, experiences, and pasts. Love for myself and all that I have grown through.

At six years old, I was his "Little Bit" and his "brown-eyed girl." Today, no matter how much I have changed or how our relationship would have evolved, I know I would still be the same in his eyes, and I no longer need to prove that to anyone—not even me.

4

KEEP GOING

———

I don't think Amanda was born with an old soul;
I think when Dad died, it simply grew up.

Too nervous to turn around, Amanda kept her eyes forward, shaky and much too on edge for an eleven-year-old on a regular summer day.

A year passed since our father was shot and killed, but Amanda started to feel his presence, repeatedly and inexplicably.

It made her uneasy.

"Mom, sometimes I…I get scared Dad's behind me," Amanda said. "I keep worrying he's there."

"Oh honey, you should talk to your therapist about that this week," Mom said. "I'm sure she'd be able to help."

———

Amanda was born in 1987 to teenage parents Shelley and her high school boyfriend Steve.[1]

By the time Shelley found out she was pregnant with Amanda though, her relationship with Steve was on the outs. He tried to be involved but quickly determined neither the relationship nor this belly flop into fatherhood was right for him.

Lucky for Shelley and Amanda, someone else was in the picture: Shelley's best friend Bob.

Her relationship with Bob grew once Amanda was in the picture—not just in friendship, but also in love. By this time, Shelley and Steve split, and Shelley and Bob came together as one.

Three years after Amanda was born, Shelley and Bob got married; two short months later, in May 1991, they had me.

Realizing just how much Bob loved and cared for Amanda, Steve decided to remit his rights as her parental guardian and signed them over to Bob.

Bob was happy to take on that responsibility. So, on July 21, 1993, just before Amanda entered kindergarten, he adopted Amanda as his own, and we spent four, chaotic, blissful years together as a family of four.

We moved from Massachusetts to New Hampshire and back again, and barely got by on Hamburger Helper and sloppy joes while Mom and Dad started their lives and landscaping business together.

We started school, made new friends, and squeezed in weekly Italian Sunday suppers. We were normal, and we were happy.

But almost as quickly as it started, it all came crashing down.

One month after Dad died, Amanda and I found ourselves in our first therapy session together.

We walked into a small office filled with toys, including a bright yellow *Rock'em Sock'em Robots* set sitting on a table.

"Hi girls," said the woman. "My name is Jane."[2]

Jane, who had short, straight brunette hair and a soft smile, reached out to Mom just after learning about Dad's death. She knew people at the preschool where Mom worked and was quick to offer her services. Mom knew we would need more support, and so did she. So, when help sought her out, she welcomed the call.

Sitting on Jane's office floor playing Scrabble, that day and for many weeks to follow, Amanda felt safe.

"There was something about that floor," Amanda said. "It offered me a sense of comfort and connection. A place where I was grounded. It's the emotions I remember and how I fondly I look back on those moments, not because of what was said, but because of how it all made me feel."

Amanda loved Dad as her own, but she always knew her biological father was out there, somewhere, living and breathing and going about his life without her.

While I grappled with the loss of one father, my sister grieved two—unable to shake the way both made her feel rejected.

Unworthy, she thought. *Forever alone.*

"I couldn't face these feelings too long, and I don't remember talking about them specifically with Jane," said Amanda. "I kept them at a distance and just kept going."

Into herself and away from what happened, Amanda became quiet and withdrawn, scared of a world that could continue to take from her.

"I retreated," she said.

Amanda gravitated to the physical places she knew—her elementary school and her gymnastics gym. She sought comfort and routine in the adults who created safe spaces for her outside of her home —first Jane, then a teacher, and a longtime gymnastics coach.

When it was time to enter high school, Amanda was terrified. The people she relied on for so long could not come with her. She'd have to do this on her own.

"I was painfully shy and dreaded every second," she said. "I ate bagels every day for lunch because I was too nervous to figure out how any of the other lunch lines worked. I didn't want kids to look at me or notice me, and when it came time to eat, I'd leave the cafeteria and sit alone in the atrium, scared to talk to anyone."

In the tenth grade, though, Amanda got a new, brave feeling of curiosity.

At home one day after school, Amanda approached Mom.

"I think I want to look into learning about my biological father," she told her. Amanda didn't know what finally sparked this desire, but it was there. Her gut was telling her to go for it.

"Okay...sure. Let's do this," said Mom, surprised yet supportive.

Feeling determined, Amanda was excited by Mom's response. She thought they'd start slow, do some research together and then someday reach out, but Mom jumped on the opportunity to help Amanda find answers.

"I got it! I contacted Steve's sister, who gave me his number. Oh also, kind of big news," said Mom to Amanda, nervously. "His sister told me a lot about your family. You have a half-brother! And there's also your biological aunt's life partner, and their three kids. Your cousins, technically, I guess..."

It was a lot, and because everyone seemed so excited by this connection, the group decided to meet.

Not long after, Amanda found herself standing with Mom on her biological aunt Sarah's doorstep.[3] Amanda was wearing her favorite khaki-colored corduroy pants and light pink t-shirt, already covered in sweat.

Sarah welcomed them in, and Amanda quickly realized they were the first ones there. Sarah's partner and their three kids sat in the living room, smiling awkwardly, and offered them a seat while they waited for Amanda's half-brother John.[4]

Amanda was a nervous wreck and welcomed the distraction when Sarah handed her photos of John as a child.

"I sat there thinking, *I missed an entire world. How unfair is it that I didn't get to be a part of this in some way?* I love being a big sister, and I would have loved to be his as well," she recalled.

Then in walked John. For the first time in her life, she felt a feeling of, maybe not belonging, but relatability.

Holy crap. He looks just like me, she thought. For Amanda, this was an anomaly because our brother Nick and I look like twins, and nothing like her.

Amanda and John exchanged niceties and looked through photos together. They gave each other their numbers and played with his cousins while the adults caught up on life.

They also opened up about their experience with their shared biological father.

Amanda told John about how she sent Steve a high school photo and a brief note when Mom got his contact information from their aunt. "I never heard back," she said, deflated.

"That's because he's never going to be a dad," John assured her. He too had tried to reach out and failed, one too many times to count.

After that meeting, Amanda and John tried to stay in touch with each other, but as shy as she was and him just the same, they found it difficult to connect on much more than shared genes and bad dad experiences.

What am I doing wrong? Amanda wondered. *What did I do to deserve this…to not be able to keep these people in my life?*

The loss of each father was different, but the feelings were similar. This experience offered Amanda a taste of closure but compounded her constant feeling of rejection.

That same tenth grade year, Amanda met her classmate Amy. Bubbly and boisterous, Amy owned the room. Lucky for Amanda, she found her way into her orbit.

"To this day, Amy and I joke that our child study teacher made her become my friend because I didn't have any," Amanda said.

They became best friends and, both interested in children's education, applied to the same colleges.

Together, they went to Southern New Hampshire University, and there, off on her own yet still within Amy's supportive reach, Amanda began to thrive.

"I remember giving myself pep talks," she said. *You are worthy. People deserve to know you. You don't need to be afraid of anyone anymore.* Over and over, walking that campus, she'd repeat these words in her head.

Amanda thought she wanted to be an elementary school teacher like Amy, but after her first semester at college, she realized it wasn't for her.

"I did a yearlong stint as a student teacher in high school and loved it but came to learn I did not like classroom management. I wanted to work one-on-one with kids," Amanda said.

She pursued an undergraduate degree in child development with a minor in psychology and became fascinated with human development and behavior. In 2010, Amanda started her master's degree in social work at the University of New Hampshire.

After her very first day of classes, she called Mom, elated.

"I have never been more sure of what I wanted to do with my life than I am right now," said Amanda.

During her master's program, she got the opportunity to try out a variety of career paths, including early intervention, new parenting skills, and school counseling.

In her final placement, she worked directly with kids on social issues, bullying, substance use, and home stressors.

"This is when I realized I wanted to work with kids in schools," said Amanda. "Kids can be so distracted by outside factors they don't have the ability to focus on academics. They just need someone to realize that for them and to offer a little help."

After a few years in the field, bouncing around from one tough in-home social work job to another, Amanda got an opportunity to join a large agency in the North Shore where she lived.

Nearing her thirtieth birthday and ready for a change of pace, Amanda eagerly accepted.

When she was clearing out her office, one of her co-workers approached.

"Just curious, will you also be working for Jane Brown?" she asked.

"...What? How do you know that name? Wait," Amanda said. She instantly reached out to her friend Erin who also worked for the new company.

"Is Jane Brown the same Jane you've been referring to all of these years as your mentor?" Amanda asked.

"Yes!" Erin said.

Impossible, Amanda thought.

Yet indeed, she looked her up and it was the same Jane Brown—her childhood therapist. Approximately twenty years after seeing Amanda as a patient, Jane became her boss in the same line of work.

Our family always jokes that Amanda has an old soul.

But it wasn't until this moment of reflection between me and my sister, in finding meaning in our stories—how they differed and how we fared—that I've come to a new conclusion.

I don't think Amanda was born with an old soul; I think when Dad died, it simply grew up.

Now, Amanda is on a pursuit to help kids like her find their way back to themselves and back to their childhood—to learn not to run and shield and protect, but to feel and to grow, just like Jane and her other mentors did for her.

"I play that same game of Scrabble with my patients together on the floor," said Amanda. "That's what I want to be for people that need it. A place to feel grounded. That's why I do what I do."

5

PERPENDICULAR PATHS

———

*The dichotomy and likeness of our
two situations collided over eggs and coffee
and a belief that together we could do some good.*

When I walked into Bobby C's restaurant in Melrose, Massachusetts on January 29, 2017, Greg Gibson was waiting for me by the bar.

I had spent the last forty-five minutes alone in my car, driving out from my Natick apartment to an unfamiliar town, glaring at every opportunity to turn around. My pounding heart told me to press on, but my introverted brain was doing everything in its power to convince my heart otherwise.

I walked through the front doors to the smell of bacon and the bustling sounds of brunch on a Sunday morning.

These are strangers. This is strange. Who do you think you are? Didn't Mom ever teach you anything? My mind was racing, but my gut stood still.

Never had I done anything like this. I mean, to this day, I have never even been on a blind date. And while this was definitely not a date, I was going in blind and alone. But it felt right.

Following less than a handful of email exchanges with members of the Everytown Survivors Network, a gun violence support and advocacy group, I was invited out to brunch. It was a chance for members, old and new, to meet up, hear stories, and talk about gun sense advocacy plans and ideas for a long year ahead.

Before my anxiety got the best of me, we made eye contact.

The then-seventy-one-year-old from Gloucester, Massachusetts had thick salt-and-pepper hair, glasses, and rosy, welcoming cheeks. We looked at each other as if to say, "Is that you?" And then once reassured with a smile, we made small talk, and shared in a moment of empathetic understanding for the unfortunate reasons we were there.

Because just after 10 p.m. on December 14, 1992, Greg's eighteen-year-old son Galen was shot and killed at Bard College at Simon's Rock, one of two people murdered and four more injured during one of the early reported US school shootings.

Five years later, and two and a half hours east of where his son had been shot dead, my dad was shot dead too. So began our two, long perpendicular paths of grief and growth that led to this moment in a diner in Melrose, Massachusetts.

I finally met Greg, who had longed for his son, and he met me, still longing for my father. The dichotomy and likeness of our two situations—a parent still grieving a child and a child still grieving a parent—collided over eggs and coffee and a belief that together we could do some good.

Determined to at least come off as if I knew what I was talking about and that I could prove useful to this group of veteran gun sense advocates, I researched as many of them as I could before I arrived. I read what stories I could find, from news articles to social media posts, and I took notes on current gun violence statistics and the political issues of the day.

I walked into that restaurant knowing Greg's story best.

In Greg's book, *Gone Boy: A Father's Search for the Truth in His Son's Murder*, he describes the morning after Galen was killed and how details of the shooting slowly trickled in.

Greg learned that members of Galen's college administration were made aware of a suspicious package addressed to a student from company called Classic Arms. Without enough knowledge about the legality of opening a student's package or what this company sold, they allowed it to be passed along to the student unopened. The college had received an anonymous tip that evening that a student had a gun and might use it.

Yet the police were never called, and the administration's subsequent actions would prove too slow. Before anyone at the college decided to approach the student in question, he began walking through the small, remote campus, shooting at random.

> *First he shot and seriously wounded the guard at the front gate. Then he murdered a professor driving past. Then he walked to the library, where he murdered Galen and wounded another student. Then he wounded two more students. Then, somehow, he surrendered and was arrested, unharmed. His name was Wayne Lo (Gibson, 1999).*

Greg and his family's grief took on a much more accelerated yet, for me, eerily familiar form.

> *What energy was left over from grieving, we put into being "normal." ...In our depleted state, normal life led*

*us and not the other way around. When it said smile,
we smiled. When it said talk, we talked. it told us when
to sleep and rise and work and eat (Gibson, 1999).*

From the outside looking in, according to Greg, this is what
you'd see. A family picking up the pieces, learning to be a
smaller family. Behind the scenes though, Greg was on a
quest for answers, motivated by a budding determination
to keep this from happening to anyone else. To any other
family.

He went to the college and met with the very administration that failed their son. He asked his questions, and
even though he didn't like the answers—each resulting in
an entirely new question—it gave him what he needed next.
It gave him fodder for a lawsuit against the college, for ret-
ribution, for holding everyone accountable, and for what
happened to Galen on that December day.

Greg and his family wished for both Wayne Lo and the
college's leadership to take ownership and responsibility over
the senselessness of their son's murder.

Lo received the guilty verdict they had hoped for—in
the first degree, twice—and would spend the rest of his life
in prison without chance of parole. But their son's college
wouldn't find themselves in the same sort of shackled pre-
dicament. According to Greg in his book, they wouldn't own
up to their role in Galen's death and he would find himself
lost in a civil suit that never seemed to end.

*I waited, with increasing discomfort, while our lawyers
prepared their case against the people at the college. My
discomfort arose from the surprising fact that, despite
the passage of time, I was not getting over Galen's*

death… I was not finding peace…I had turned it all over to the judicial system, and I was counting on them to do it for me. The problem was, they were taking their sweet time about it, and I was suffering (Gibson, 1999).

The college's insurance company tried to settle with the Gibson family for $250,000. But Greg and his family never wanted money. They only wished for public accountability, and it was clear it wouldn't happen. Years passed, and the legal system found new and different ways to stall Greg's progress.

Wayne Lo was locked up. There was nothing more I could do about him. But I was furious (at college leadership) for the way they'd handled things on the day of the shootings…Now I thought I could see a solution. I'd write a book (Gibson, 1999).

I read these words years before writing this book, and I just happened to read them again while writing it. I don't think it was a coincidence. Maybe I stored his words somewhere deep in my subconscious, and when ready, they said, *Psst … look here. If he can do it, so can you.*

Because I believe in the power of storytelling. It's not until we see the world through someone else's eyes and try to feel what they've felt that we can attempt to understand where they've come from and walk alongside them in whichever way they're growing.

That day in Bobby C's restaurant, I now know I had one real goal in mind: watch and learn.

Between our few in-person interactions, email exchanges, and the four times I've read his book, Greg has become a sort of role model in my life.

He's taught me, whether he knows it or not, that each and every one of us has a unique ability to raise awareness and make a positive impact. Some people I've met on this journey are incredible with spoken word—they speak at rallies and testify against pro-gun bills in court. Others are running for local office to bring gun sense efforts into their state politics.

Then, there are people like Greg and me—better with written word, finding our voice and place among the noise all the same.

Townies at heart, soft yet sarcastic, never loud but heard when we want to be. Family driven, writers, and determined as all heck. Both of us just trying to find the best ways to use our fire for the purpose of change.

If Greg can make this much of an impact on me—just by welcoming me in, responding to my emails, and writing his book—then I can do the same for someone else.

I can put myself out there and I can do this too.

In his latest efforts to use his story for good, Greg did what many couldn't bear to do. He talked to his son's killer, Wayne Lo, first through written word, and then in person. He listened. And he came up with a plan that would involve the support, engagement, and partnership of Lo himself.

According to Isabel Dobrin and Michael Garofalo of NPR, who covered the story in 2017, this unlikely pair teamed up, not for the purpose of forgiveness or closure, but to put much-needed weight behind the importance of gun sense measures in this country.

Having suffered a psychological break on the night of the shooting, Lo was open about the fact that if he had not been able to purchase a gun so easily, he might not have done what he did at all. Together, they made a short documentary about what happened on the day in 1992, how Lo was able to commit his crimes, and why they believe the world needs to hear this issue from both sides (Gibson, 2019).

While Greg continues to push forth, he still questions if any of it's enough.

"I spent years convinced that if I share this story with the rest of the world, they'll see the sense in common sense gun laws...I find out that I'm wrong," said Greg (Gibson, 2019).

"But what if he's not?" wrote *The Boston Globe*'s Nestor Ramos after watching the documentary. "The video is four minutes and forty-three seconds long. It took twenty-five years of grief and loss to produce. And all Greg Gibson asks is that you watch it."

GETTING INVOLVED

Moms Demand Action for Gun Sense in America has become a beacon in my life, like a big bat signal calling me home.

Just out of college, at my first job as a PR associate at a small firm outside of Boston, I found myself publicizing the Baskin' Robbins flavor of the month and making sure the Dunkin' Donuts Cuppy mascot would be on time for my client's ribbon cutting. It wasn't bad work per se, but I had no idea where this job would take me.

A couple of years into the job, feeling what I assumed to be boredom coupled with an inability to keep up with my rent, I applied for another PR job—this time with my alma mater, Babson College.

I got the offer and excitedly accepted. Two years after walking away from that college as a graduate, I'd be heading back to promote its brand, and I was thrilled.

What I didn't know then was it wasn't actually boredom that pushed me from my first job, nor would it be the reason those same feelings bubbled to the surface a couple years into my next one.

I had a desire to spend my energy elsewhere, and on matters I cared about more. I wanted to be better involved in the gun sense effort.

From age twenty-one to twenty-nine, I got promoted five times collectively by two employers. I impressed myself with my new communications skills, landing notable media placements and running a total of six brand social media accounts. I wrote countless articles, scripted some pretty cool videos, and had my hands in major campaigns and events.

It's clear to me only now that I've figured out how to balance my volunteer work with my career, that my apathy toward my jobs was never due to lack of interest in the companies or positions. It always has been, and will be, about wanting to use my skills to save people from experiencing what my family was dealt. To help put an end to gun violence in America.

Near the end of 2016, just after Donald Trump was elected president, I had an idea. Likely sparked by the chaos that ensued after that election and the realization that an NRA-supported Republican would soon hold the most powerful position in the world, I felt a burning desire to double down on my hatred for this country's gun sense issues.

What am I good at? What do I love? How can I turn all of that into action?

I spent the weeks between the election and New Years on Google. Much like other times in my life, I turned to the internet when I craved answers. Yet unlike those times, I found a lot of people just like me.

According to Everytown for Gun Safety, New York City Mayor Michael Bloomberg, Boston Mayor Thomas Menino, and thirteen other mayors co-founded Mayors Against Illegal Guns in 2006. Moms Demand Action entered the scene after some great legislative successes, including the defeat of an NRA-backed bill that would have forced every state to recognize every other state's concealed carry permits.

In 2012, one day after the terrible slaying of twenty-six people, including twenty children, at Sandy Hook Elementary School in Newtown, Connecticut, then stay-at-home mom Shannon Watts launched Moms Demand Action. The organization called for moms everywhere to do more than offer thoughts and prayers.

It wouldn't take long for the two organizations to realize their collective power, including a continued surge in supporters and volunteers. In 2013, the pair came together to form a parent organization called Everytown for Gun Safety—the largest gun violence prevention organization in America. Today, the organization includes Moms Demand Action, Mayors Against Illegal Guns, Students Demand Action (formed after the Parkland, Florida shooting in February 2018), and the Everytown Survivor Network, a nationwide community of survivors working together to end gun violence. (Everytown for Gun Safety, 2021)

And that survivor network caught my eye because I had never used that word—survivor—to describe myself.

According to the organization, a survivor is anyone who has experienced gun violence. This includes those who have been personally threatened or wounded with a gun, have witnessed an act of gun violence, or have had someone they know wounded or killed by a gun.

> *People may use different words to describe living through gun violence: Some may use "victim," others may use "survivor." Some use neither. Knowing that each person experiences trauma and healing differently, we use the word "survivor" to acknowledge pain and resilience—and to recognize the unacceptable daily consequences of gun violence that are the reality for too many Americans (Everytown Support Fund, 2021).*

Just like realizing what I've gone through is trauma, allowing myself to say, "I'm a survivor," and seeing this organization say it too—it gave me something new; a sort of validator I didn't know I needed in order to raise my voice.

Now, I don't need to qualify my desire to end gun violence by being a survivor of gun violence. What I've come to realize is that one too many times, I've let that little self-conscious voice in the back of my head say, "You don't know what you're doing. Who do you think you are? Let someone else do it."

Under the example and leadership of advocates like Greg, I've realized I don't have to be an expert or professionally involved in the organization to create change. I also now know an entire network of people is out there to support me, and that is all the validation I needed to jump in.

In December 2016, when I reached out to the Everytown for Gun Safety to inquire about the Survivor Network, Greg Gibson became my springboard.

Incredibly welcoming and enthusiastic about my inquiry, Greg quickly connected me with Moms Demand Action

Massachusetts. Before I knew it, I found myself at that restaurant in Melrose, sitting around a table with ten other survivors of gun violence, nervously pitching an idea I had then about a charity-driven music festival to help younger generations get involved in the cause.

"I would call it Birthdays Over Bullets, or B.O.B. Fest, in honor of my father, Bob DiPietro, who was killed by gun violence when I was six," I said. "A musician himself, I can think of no better way to honor his life, and the lives and would-be birthdays of so many others, than with a birthday party in the form of a really cool music festival."

"I love this idea," said one of the survivors from a few seats down, who I had noticed leaning in excitedly as I shared my story.

"Me too," said another, who then handed me her card. "Put this idea into a proposal, and let's stay in touch," she added.

I was jazzed and quite honestly the most fulfilled I had felt in a long time just knowing there may be something I could do with the skillset I had acquired to help make a difference.

Then, another dream of mine came true.

I got pregnant, which I was actively trying to do with the help of infertility treatments. Once the treatments started, I didn't think everything would happen so quickly, but it did, and again, I was thrilled.

I spent the next three months nauseous as all heck, and then six months elated, growing, and nesting.

I thought, *I'll pick B.O.B. Fest and my volunteerism up next year. It's not, not happening. It's just not happening now, and that's okay.*

In May 2018, I had my beautiful baby girl, and my marriage fell apart that very same year.

Sometimes I let my own negative thoughts get in the way.

Is it all an excuse? Have I let life and the unexpected be my reason not to pursue my dreams?

No. That's just what life is. It presents you with the unexpected—both in the form of miracles and in pain, but it doesn't ever have to be forever.

I believe it just wasn't the right time to get heavily involved in the cause, and that's okay. I got a taste, and I realized I had found a community all my own.

Now, I'm ready to enter my thirties with a renewed sense of self, finally using my personal and professional skillsets toward something I care so deeply about.

6

STILL

I don't regret a second of it.
The falling in love or the being in love.
Not even the falling out of it.

In ninety-five-degree heat on the afternoon of July 15, 2016, I stood in front of two old, white-painted church doors. My right arm was intertwined with the left arm of my eighteen-year-old brother Nick.

I could feel the weight of the fake eyelashes glued on my eyes two hours before, and the sweat dripping down my back I was hoping no one would see.

I wiggled my toes anxiously in my new stilettos and gripped my beautiful bouquet of lilies in my left hand while fiddling with my parents' gold wedding bands that were tied around the front.

"Are you ready?" asked Claire, my peppy wedding coordinator, smiling eagerly at me with one hand on the door.

"I guess," I whispered excitedly and looked up to meet Nick's big, brown eyes.

The doors opened. Then, one hundred people who filled the pews of this small Catholic church in Westerly, Rhode Island, stood up, almost all at once.

I couldn't see him at first, but I heard the piano and our song start to play in instrumental.

I sang along in my head. *I want to call you mine. I want to hold your hand forever and never let you forget it.*

When I thought my heart couldn't feel fuller, he stepped into view in front of the priest who was wearing a long white robe at the end of the aisle adorned with my father's favorite flower, the dogwood.

He looked at me, smiled, and wiped a visible tear from his cheek.

In this moment, I thought all was right in the world.

We stood hand-in-hand, me in the sleek, white satin dress I spent a year designing with a seamstress, him in a grey tux, grey tie, and sharp oak shoes we picked out together. Though everyone looked on, all I saw was him.

"Do you take this woman to be your lawful wedded wife, to have and to hold from this day forward, for better or for worse, for richer or for poorer, in sickness and in health, to love and to cherish until death do you part?" asked the priest to my fiancé.

"I do," he said.

"Do you take this man to be your lawful wedded husband, to have and to hold from this day forward, for better or for worse, for richer or for poorer, in sickness and in health, to love and to cherish until death do you part?" asked the priest to me.

"I do," I said.

"You may now kiss your bride," said the priest.

On February 9, 2019, I woke after a restless night of sleep.

Scared and alone on one side of our queen bed that I had slept in for the last seven years, I tried to focus on everything I'd need to do, rather than what I was leaving behind.

"What time is your family getting here?" he asked quietly from the kitchen, holding our nine-month-old daughter.

"Eight. My mom and Michael will be here first with the truck, then my sister, and some friends will follow," I said.

"Okay. I will take the baby to get breakfast and maybe for a walk...I can help, you know. I don't mind," he said.

"No. I have to do this on my own," I said, my voice breaking.

He packed the baby's backpack with supplies as I taped my last boxes shut. I kissed her forehead and cried.

Crying was just something we all got used to.

We looked each other in the eyes, and he pulled me in as if to say goodbye forever.

Even though we'd see each other in passing for the rest of our daughter's life—at court, at drop offs, at sporting and school events, at birthdays, and graduation—this would be the last time we'd spend in *our* home. This would be our last hug as a family and our last goodbye as *us*.

I ugly cried, and I gasped for air, and then we both pushed away.

Not long after he left, my parents rushed up the four flights of stairs that led to my apartment with more boxes, and tape, and that dreaded look of sympathy I was hoping we'd all avoid. Behind them followed my aunt, uncle, sister, and six of my closest friends.

In under thirty minutes, we had all my belongings in five separate cars and followed one another like a funeral procession to my new apartment ten minutes away.

It had been forty days since he first uttered the word divorce, and maybe thirty days since the reality set in that we were actually going through with it.

In the rush of the movers and boxes and emotions, I reflected on the day I told my family we were done. They stared at me, shocked, in the living room of my childhood home.

"You and the baby can move in here," said my mom. I just shook my head. I knew I had their support, in whatever way I needed it, but I wanted to manage this. I didn't want my entire life to change. I wasn't quite ready to lose control of it all.

I sent countless apartment inquiries, visited quite a few, and got rejected from the first four I applied to. One real estate agent even had the nerve to ask me, "Are you sure you want to do this?" after reviewing my single debt-to-income ratio. "What choice do you think I have?" I replied.

My soon-to-be ex-husband found the Craigslist ad that led to my first post-divorce apartment.

How kind, I thought. I looked at what he sent me because I was desperate. I applied on the spot because it was perfect.

The swirl of loved ones carrying my personal belongings from their cars into this adorable, one bedroom apartment on a cold, sunny day—it's both a blur and a bittersweet memory. In and out at lightning speed, everyone hyper-focused on the task at hand.

Help her get settled. Make her feel at home. Show her how much she's loved.

For that, I am forever indebted to them (you know who you are, and I love you with all my heart).

I remember the sinking nausea that crept in as more and more of my things found their new home and some of my many movers started running out of things to do besides stare.

Then, a large flower delivery showed up at my new door.

I opened the card. "I love you! Love always, Alex," it read, from my best friend who lived 3,000 miles away. I burst into tears, and the friends who were there with me all rushed up to me and hugged me together.

It hit me, everything, all at once. My friends and family, near and far, they knew I was going through hell, and they knew all I needed to hear from them was, "I love you."

Heading into this new chapter with their support, I knew the rest was up to me.

A month later, on March 19, 2019, we drove separately, from our two apartments located seven minutes apart, to the Middlesex Probate Court.

I got there first, after dropping our then-ten-month-old off at daycare.

In the fourth outfit I tried on that morning, because everything was falling off my body after the stress weight I had lost, I walked into this grand, marble-filled building early that Tuesday morning.

I was unsure of where to go or if I should wait for him to arrive. I walked up to the desk underneath a large "Information" sign.

"I have a court appointment…for divorce," I said, hesitantly, to the woman looking back at me.

"You're going to want to go up three flights and check-in. They will have you fill out paperwork together, and then, once approved, you will be assigned to a time to enter the courtroom and see the judge," she said.

I turned to see him entering the same door I had, looking fidgety and avoiding eye contact with me at all costs.

"Do you know where we need to go?" he asked.

"Yeah," I said and began to walk upstairs.

In a DMV-esque room, we were handed a stack of paperwork and pointed to a table to fill it all out.

"Bring it back when it's complete. You'll need your licenses and a credit card or check," said the woman. She never looked me in the eye. And she never stood at that desk long enough to start a conversation.

We sat across from one another; me filling out the paperwork; him answering my questions as I went along. He crosschecked each answer with the papers we had signed off on together in a mediator's office over the last two months.

Once we handed the stack of paper across the court's desk and paid our dues for bothering the state with our failed marriage, we were pointed down a hallway where we were told to wait until the judge called us in.

Not too long after, two big brown doors creaked open. Without a word, we were waved in by a security guard, but so was the entire line of people behind us.

We were shuffled into a crowded pew. The judge, dressed in a long, black robe, raised her hand and called two names that weren't ours.

I watched as a woman walked from one side of the courtroom to the front, and a man walked from the other side to meet her there. But they did not turn to each other.

"Do you swear to tell the truth, the whole truth, and nothing but the truth?" the judge asked.

"I do," they both said.

It took a few seconds for me to realize this wouldn't be any sort of special occasion nor a private matter.

My heart sunk as I listened to the woman answer the judge's questions about the renovations she was doing to her house, which used to be their house, and the contractor's she owed, and the legal battles that have long ensued between her and her estranged husband standing next to her.

I kept looking between the couple on the stand, to the fifty strangers sitting behind them, and to the man beside me who today would officially become my ex-husband.

"This is horrible," I whispered, unsure if he heard me.

An hour or more passed before the judge finally read our names from the papers a court official had just handed her.

We walked to the front of the room. My legs were trembling. I was sweaty and I was cold.

"Do you swear to tell the truth, the whole truth, and nothing but the truth?" the judge asked.

"I do," said my husband.

I simply nodded.

"Ma'am, I need a verbal response from you to each of my questions," said the judge.

"I do," I said, so quietly I still don't think she heard me. She moved on.

The judge put on her glasses and started reading our paperwork.

"According to your separation agreement, you're filing for divorce due to an 'irretrievable breakdown of your marital relationship.' Is this correct?" she asked.

"Yes," said my husband, quickly.

"...Yeah," I said, not as sure.

"There is a young child, age ten months. You plan to co-parent equally, and you have worked with a mediator on a parenting agreement and schedule?" said the judge.

"Yes," he said.

"Yes," I said, now crying, visibly, audibly, and very publicly.

She read through the rest of our documents, signed her name at the end, and passed a sheet of paper along through a court official, for each of us to sign.

"Your marriage is dissolved today, March 19, 2019. You're free to go," she said.

By the time we got divorced, we had been together for seven years. Six of those years were bliss, or so I thought.

But then came something more real than either of us had ever experienced. A belly, a baby, and responsibility like we'd never known.

While I spent most of that final year watching my body grow, I didn't see past it to notice a change in him, nor the quiet way he walked away.

Between her birth in May of 2018 and our divorce just under one year later, I found myself in a desperate and depressing state. I grasped at every last bit of the relationship I held so dear, convinced I could make it work.

Our baby I knew he wanted and adored. Our marriage, it quickly became clear, he did not.

Though he already gave up on us, I was ready to fight until the death to keep our relationship intact for her.

So, I told almost no one what was going on.

I tried therapy, in secrecy. I posted photos and cute captions about our little family. And in front of anyone else, I painted on my very best smile.

Whenever we'd get home from being out or with family, I could feel the stale, awkward tension in the air. I cried a lot. He questioned how long we could go on this way. And I kept pushing us and him to try harder. To be better.

It didn't work.

Looking back, there's something that my father's death has given me, and that is a sense of urgency for life, and especially for love.

Feeling a sense of urgency—to do, to act, to never miss out, because who knows how short this life is—it's brought me some of my highest highs and my lowest lows. This divorce being one of those lows.

Just after turning twenty, I met my ex-husband on my dream trip to live halfway across the world in Australia for six months by myself. I was fresh out of an intense high school relationship, craving the world.

I wanted to see well beyond my purview, to meet new people. What I didn't know was I'd meet *this* person. Someone who I'd first get close with as a friend and then pretty quickly fall madly in love with.

I don't regret a second of it. The falling in love or the being in love. Not even the falling out of it.

The first two brought me extreme happiness, life experiences, adventure, and most importantly, my child. And that last bit, it brought me a whole lot of perspective—about what's most important in life, how strong I am independently, for me and my baby, and that things always have a way of getting better, if you let them.

When I knew that my marriage was over, and there was no saving the family I worked for, it was like I tucked that piece of my life snuggly into bed—not completely out of sight—but with some peace of mind, and the tiring weight of it all lifted from my shoulders.

I can do this, I thought. That confidence, I believe, came from that same sense of urgency for life. From looking back on my family's healing and growth after Dad's death. From being able to see hope, opportunity and second chances.

I was divorced at twenty-seven. So what? I had so much life left to live, and I needed to pick myself up and get back at it. I was glad that if this had to happen, it happened to me and my daughter, so young. She would never know any different, and I could move on.

I took a hard look in the mirror and reminded myself repeatedly of everything I loved about me, inside and out. Then, I let myself go be that person. I learned to love my life again, just the way it was.

It helps that in doing that—in simply being me, and a happy me at that—I reconnected with a friend who would make a quick and extremely positive impact on my life.

Now, I don't think the answer to every broken heart is to find someone else to mend it. I've made that mistake before too and sometimes, it just doesn't work; but this friend and I caught up, talked day and night, and even went to get spontaneous tattoos together right around the time of my divorce.

For the first time in a long time, my smile wasn't forced.

I've since let this amazing human into our life. I let him tell me he loves me, and I've said it back every day since.

I learned to trust again because he and I deserve that. And I refused to let my fears—of things going wrong or of anyone questioning my decisions—hinder the amazing relationship that found me and my daughter.

Because those fears that we tend to worry about—they don't account for what I've lived through, how happy I am now, or how I've come alive again because I've allowed myself the space to do so.

7

DRIPS ON A ROCK

———

And the glimmer of hope that she would feel,
thinking that, someday,
somebody somewhere
would do something.

Shannon Watts was home alone in Zionsville, Indiana just before midday on Friday, December 14, 2012.

I had read this story before—in articles, on her organization's website, in her book—but hearing it for the first time directly from her, on a phone call just between the two of us… hit different.

Shannon's husband had a day full of meetings, and her five children were in school, her son in middle school and her four daughters spread between high school and college.

Then a forty-one-year-old stay-at-home mom and consultant, Shannon was cleaning up after a week of shepherding her little humans in and out of the house for their daily routines and looking forward to the weekend ahead.

Like most mornings, Shannon turned on her television and clicked over to the news. It was something her former public relations brain turned to like a compass arrow constantly spinning north.

"We have breaking news today out of Newtown, Connecticut, where sources say multiple people have been shot at an elementary school," said an anchor.

Shannon stood, immovable. From the anchors' somber faces to scenes of very small children being marched out of their school. The bad news poured out slowly, and then all at once.

"Our helicopter is live from Sandy Hook Elementary School...where...we're seeing...those are officers with guns drawn running into the wooded area behind the school... we're unsure of any casualties at this time but will keep you updated as we learn more," said one of the anchors.

"Please, God, don't let this be as bad as it seems," said Shannon to herself, out loud.

Just before 1 p.m., the headline that ran across the anchors desk changed.

"More than twenty people, most of them children, killed in elementary shooting," it read.

By 1:10 p.m., that number read twenty-six.

The anchors' faces were pale, and so was Shannon's. She pushed the pile of laundry aside, sat down on her bed, and covered her face with her hands.

School and other mass shootings were an all-too-familiar scene in the news cycle of Shannon's life. People running out of buildings, scared to the core, with their hands above their heads on loop.

The first one she could remember happened on Wednesday, October 16, 1991.

Shannon was twenty years old and home alone in her parents' house in Plano, Texas. While watching *CNN*, a breaking news alert filled the screen.

"Twenty-three people have been killed after a gunman drove his pickup through a Luby's cafeteria window and opened fire on more than 150 diners today in Killeen, Texas. An additional twenty-seven people have been injured. The gunman is presumed dead. Stay with us for updates," said the anchor.

Shannon heard the telephone ring, and pulled herself, but not her eyes, away from the TV.

She picked up the phone.

"Hi...Shannon?" said her father. She realized he didn't yet know about what happened in the diner. Before she could say anything, she burst into tears.

From that massacre in 1991, to the Columbine shooting in 1999, and the Virginia Tech shooting in 2007, the record in Shannon's brain was far too long. She remembers them all like they were yesterday.

She also remembers the gut-sinking feeling she gets each time she learns of all the lives lost and impacted and the glimmer of hope she would feel thinking that, someday, somebody somewhere would do something.

Nothing ever changed. "I realized on the day of the Sandy Hook tragedy that it was up to us," Shannon told me.

On that December day, she stared at the devastated faces of family members strewn across her television screen. First heartbroken, then enraged, she thought to herself, "How can our systems and laws that are supposed to protect these children have so clearly failed? If they aren't safe in their schools, they aren't safe anywhere."

"Why does this keep happening?" she said, again to herself, out loud.

In her debut book, *Fight Like a Mother*, Shannon describes this breaking point: "Enough waiting for legislators to pass better gun laws. Enough hoping that things would somehow get better...Enough complacency. Enough standing on the sidelines," (Watts, 2019).

The day after the Sandy Hook shooting, eight hundred miles away from the tragedy that occurred twenty-four hours before, Shannon tried to ease her mind.

Reluctantly, Shannon wrote, she got in her car and headed for a local yoga class. Once settled in the studio, she sat in hero pose and listened to the heavy breathing of her classmates.

She squeezed her eyes shut and tried to find balance. But all she could think about were those kids and the pundits she'd seen on the morning news offering their condolences without ever mentioning a call for change.

Someone has to do something, she thought, and that something wasn't yoga. Shannon stood up, rolled up her mat, and left the studio without saying a word.

In her book, she explains the light switch that went on that day in the sweaty studio. "I went online to search for support...there had to be some kind of organization already in existence—like a Mothers Against Drunk Driving for gun violence prevention...I wanted to be in the company of other women (because) ...American mothers—especially now... were afraid their children would be taken away from them. If that wasn't the type of threat that would spark a mama bear mentality, I didn't know what would," (Watts, 2019).

Shannon decided to make her own Facebook page. She had seventy-five followers at the time.

She named it "One Million Moms for Gun Control."

"You sure you want to do that?" asked her husband, John.

No big deal, she thought. "It's just a Facebook page," she said.

Then she typed the following words—words she says changed her life forever.

> *"I started this page because, as a mom, I can no longer sit on the sidelines. I am too sad and too angry. Don't let anyone tell you we can't talk about this tragedy now—they said the same after Virginia Tech, Gabby Giffords, and Aurora. The time is now." (Watts, 2019)*

With this one brave step forward and into the spotlight, Shannon launched what would very quickly become the country's first and largest grassroots movement to counter the gun lobby.

Today it is known widely as Moms Demand Action for Gun Sense in America.

Fueled by years of collective trauma from US shootings, people are coming together, for countless reasons and in tireless ways, to prevent at least one more person from getting hurt.

I wanted to be—and now believe that I am—one of those people.

Shannon Watts launched her grassroots organization by simply deciding to do *something*.

Today, this group has grown into a nonstop movement of six million gun-sense supporters with chapters in every state.

Though I was exposed to gun violence personally and through the media coverage of gun tragedies in America, it wasn't until I became involved with Moms Demand Action that I was able to quantify the pain I witnessed throughout my thirty years.

Just after the Parkland, Florida school shooting in February of 2018, fellow gun sense advocate Greg Gibson penned an opinion piece in *The New York Times* that eloquently explains the collective trauma I, he, and most likely many others, feel:

> *"When gun violence becomes commodified as content by the media, we consume it rather than experience it. As a nation, we're dead to it now. Despite our momentary hysteria, we've pretty much compartmentalized gun death, random mass shootings in particular. Consequently, we live in a country that seems to agree that 33,000 gun deaths a year is an acceptable price to pay for our unique, constitutionally guaranteed access to firearms," (The New York Times, 2018).*

According to Everytown for Gun Safety Support Fund, more than one hundred Americans die from gun violence each day and twice as many are shot and wounded.

This non-partisan organization dedicated to understanding and reducing gun violence also finds that more than half of all US adults or someone they care for have experienced gun violence in their lifetime. This country's homicide rate is twenty-five times higher than in other high-income countries (Everytown for Gun Safety Support Fund, 2021).

While 93 percent of American voters support requiring background checks on all gun sales, including 89 percent of

Republicans and 87 percent of all gun owners, 22 percent of Americans report completing their most recent gun purchase without a background check. Federal law does not yet address gun sales by unlicensed sellers (via online or gun show sales), and this loophole continues to allow people with restraining orders, a history of mental illness, and felony convictions to purchase guns without a second look (Everytown for Gun Safety Support Fund, 2021).

Moms Demand Action and organizations like Brady United Against Gun Violence, Giffords, and many local community passion projects have been instrumental in state and federal legal proceedings, corporate policy changes, and gun violence survivor and family support.

Moms Demand Action volunteers, for example, meet with and present to legislators to educate them on the consequences of passing bills that would allow permitless carry across states. They've also helped pressure companies like Facebook, Chipotle, and Target to change their in-store and user policies to protect communities and individuals from the harms of gun violence and improper sales.

In 2014, Shannon's growing group created a petition that, when signed, sent individual messages to Target's CEO asking him to create gun sense policies to protect customers in its stores. The petition was formed after photos were shared across social media of people armed with semiautomatic rifles walking through Target locations across the United States. At the time, Target did not then have any policies to stop this from happening (Everytown for Gun Safety Target Petition, 2014).

With four hundred thousand quick petition signatures, and countless social media users posting with the hashtag #OffTarget—calling for people to boycott Target nationwide—Moms Demand Action got the attention of the company's executive leadership team. And on July 2, 2014, Target announced it would ask customers not to bring guns into its stores (Moms Demand Action, 2014).

Everytown for Gun Safety, Moms Demand Action, and their supporters rally survivors and volunteers alike to campaign for gun sense candidates, meet with local legislators, support and amplify the work of local community organizations who work on similar issues, and—like in the Target example—even turn to social media en masse with hashtags that capture national attention and help to create change.

At the root of it all—every bit of effort by each and every supporter—is the trust their work, passion, individuality, needs, and ability are cared for by the people who lead them, including Shannon Watts.

It's evident in the way Shannon shows up for everyone as much as she possibly can. It became that much clearer to me after I, a brand-new author with nothing to show for it, told her my story via Instagram message and asked if she'd be willing to talk.

She quickly put me in touch with her team and said yes.

In the forty-five minutes Shannon dedicated to me, just after the 2020 election and between meetings, she continued to offer *me* words of praise and gratitude.

"In my mind, people like you, your family, and others who are activists *despite* having been impacted by gun violence—I think that's heroic," she said. "I'm not sure I could carry that pain around and be as aggressive as an activist as I am. This movement takes both of us. Those who have been impacted and those who have not. It's the same as any social issue, right? Take marriage equality, for example. You don't have to be the parent of a gay child to care about gay rights, you should just care because it's the right thing to do."

At the time, still convinced that I wasn't quite making as much of an impact as I'd like to in my volunteerism, Shannon reminded me of the important role I play as part of the collective. That a good grassroots effort thrives on the whole, not the sum of its parts.

"We have a California volunteer who coined the phrase 'naptivism.' It's this idea that even if you only have a few moments to be an activist, like when your kids are taking a nap, it matters. It makes a difference. Every call, every hashtag used on Twitter, every email. All activism is cumulative, and it's like drips on a rock," she told me.

On my own naptivist's quest, I understand now just how many ways one person, no matter their circumstance, can get shit done as long as there is a fire in their belly and a support system at their back.

"Maybe you want to run for office, or you want to change corporate policies or educate people about responsible gun storage," Shannon told me. "Dedicate even one hour a week. it will make a difference."

8

CARING FOR OUR CHILDREN

———

*Because that's really the only thing we can control.
What we choose to do with whatever time and effort and
energy we have left.*

Around 8 a.m. on January 10, 2001, nineteen-year-old
Laura Wilcox arrived at the Grass Valley, California county
Behavioral Health Department. There, she would volunteer
her time helping others—something she chose to do during
her winter break from Haverford College.

At 11:30 a.m., a forty-year-old man walked into the same
hospital building where Laura sat signing people in—on a
day when Laura chose to fill in for a colleague who was sick
and opened fire.

Halfway across the world, over 8,000 miles away, Laura's
cousin Rob Wilcox got an unexpected message from his
parents to call home immediately.

Rob was abroad in Australia during the winter break of
his final year in school. Though his family, including Laura

and their six other cousins, were scattered across the United States, they were extremely close and always carved out time to spend together, Rob recalled.

"Rob...," said his mother over the phone.

"Mom? What's wrong? Hello?" asked Rob. He could hear both of his parents fumbling to speak and he was pretty sure he could hear them crying.

"Laura's dead, Rob. She was shot!" said his mother, hysterical.

Rob was no stranger to living around gun violence having been raised in Brooklyn, New York. *But Laura? This couldn't be true.*

Her parents had long supported gun safety measures—not because they believed they were at risk themselves, in sleepy Grass Valley, California, but because they cared about stopping violence happening to others.

For Rob, guns and gun violence were just part of life.

Growing up in Brooklyn during the 1980s and 1990s, he saw shell casings in his neighborhood and the local news reported all the small acts of terror occurring around him on a daily basis. His family members even owned guns, and his father taught him to shoot as a child.

But...near Laura in her California home? No. *There's just no way a gun could have been close enough to her to hurt her*, he thought.

Rob didn't know much about what happened, but he knew he had to go home. He flew straight from Australia to California to be with his family.

It was all over the news when he arrived.

Laura was one of three killed and another three injured during a shooting spree that spanned the hospital where she worked and a restaurant down the street. According to *The*

Union newspaper, the shooting caused hours of fear in a place where cellphone ownership was uncommon, and coverage was spotty.

It took too long to figure out who was committing this act of violence, and where they went. While law enforcement rushed to figure that out, the shooter traveled from the hospital to the restaurant, shooting at random. He then fled to his nearby home while all schools and businesses remained locked down.

Later that afternoon, the shooter called his brother and admitted his guilt. Moments later, he was picked up by authorities, and his connection to the hospital was made clear immediately, since he had recently been deemed mentally ill and resisted treatment at that very facility before the shooting occurred.

In court, the shooter was found not guilty on a claim of insanity. He remains at the Napa State Hospital for the mentally ill to this day. (Kleist, 2016)

Rob remembers Laura's memorial service well. "It was a Quaker service, where people just stand up and speak when moved…There were hundreds of people," he said.

Sunlight beamed through the windows at the top of the old gymnasium. Rob tried to calm himself in the stillness of the warm air that flowed in. He watched dust particles float by through the light from above. He heard Sarah McLachlan playing softly in the background, but though he tried, none of this distracted from the sound of grief that filled the room.

Everyone was crying.

"Laura was a beautiful light, snuffed out too soon. She was successful, smart, and compassionate. The heartbreak wasn't just felt by her parents, her brothers, and our family, but also by her entire community. It was just so real and visible, how gun violence can leave such a gaping hole and have such a traumatic effect on so many people," said Rob.

He didn't know what would come next, or what exactly he could do, but he knew he wanted to do something.

Laura's parents, Rob's aunt Amanda, and Uncle Nick were not new to the gun sense movement. Before their daughter's tragic death, they were already active contributors to Brady—one of America's oldest gun violence prevention groups (Brady, 2021).

According to Rob, Amanda and Nick were pioneers in the gun sense world. Together, they took a very public stand against gun safety issues in America, and with no personal gain, spent years volunteering to save others from falling victim to gun violence.

The pair never could have imagined how close this issue would soon hit home.

Following Laura's death, Amanda and Nick got back to work. Because of their involvement, support, and their willingness to help others in honor of their daughter's life, says Rob, local legislatures were able to propose and pass Assembly Bill 1421.

A bill that became Laura's Law in 2003.

Laura's Law, new to the state of California, allows counties to provide court-ordered outpatient mental healthcare for people with severe mental illnesses who have failed to stay in treatment and who have the potential to become dangerous to themselves or others without help. (Kellar, 2020)

Amanda and Nick's dedicated work continued as they pressed for more gun safety laws.

"My aunt and uncle have had a hand in passing fifty gun sense bills that help keep people safe," said Rob. "They absolutely helped save other people. People who will never know them, who never knew Laura, but are alive now, because of them."

Rob wanted to pursue a path to do so too.

Following his cousin's death and his graduation, Rob and his girlfriend Jessa, now wife, moved to Washington, DC, to be close to the action. He found out, though, it wouldn't be as simple as he thought to get a job with a non-profit gun sense organization and to also be able to pay his bills. So, he took a job at a telemarketing firm while he tried to find the perfect opportunity, but it just wasn't there.

"You know, we came here for a reason," his girlfriend said to him, seeing Rob's frustration. "We can save money. We'll eat rice sandwiches if that's what it takes. You should do the thing that you came here to do."

She was right. He had to make it work. So, he went to Brady, where his aunt and uncle volunteered, and he told them he would do anything they needed. "I'll stuff envelopes. I don't care. I just want to help," he said.

The campaign offered to take him on as an intern on the communications team. He learned about key gun sense issues from the inside out.

"I got to work with these incredible activists across the country fighting to end gun violence. It meant so much to be making a difference and to be contributing, honoring my cousin with this work and honoring my aunt and uncle," said Rob.

All this work sparked Rob's interest in the policy side of the gun sense movement, so he applied for law school. And his girlfriend Jessa did too.

The pair went together to Northwestern and both became lawyers.

Rob's hard work allowed him the chance to work at a leading law firm, Cravath, Swaine & Moore, and the opportunity to sit on the board of directors for New Yorkers Against Gun Violence. There, he saw the benefit of gun sense educational work in schools and especially in schools that suffered from high rates of gun violence.

"We raised money to support teachers and programs that helped students become advocates on issues of gun violence directly affecting their communities. It showed me an entirely different way to work on this issue. This was about addressing the root cause and opening up doors of opportunity," said Rob.

Then, the Sandy Hook shooting happened, and it brought all the work he and his family had been doing to the national stage.

"I think gun safety is an issue that never lacked for heart or evidence. We just didn't have the power to get things done for years," said Rob. But when President Obama spoke to the nation following the shooting in Newtown, Connecticut, Rob felt a shift in the air.

We, as a nation, are left with some hard questions. Someone once described the joy and anxiety of parenthood as the equivalent of having your heart outside of your body all the time, walking around...Every parent knows there is nothing we will not do to shield our children from harm...We can't do this by ourselves...

this job of keeping our children safe, and teaching them well, is something we can only do together, with the help of friends and neighbors, the help of a community and the help of a nation...This is our first task—caring for our children. It's our first job. If we don't get that right, we don't get anything right. That's how, as a society, we will be judged. And by that measure, can we truly say, as a nation, that we are meeting our obligations? Can we honestly say that we're doing enough to keep our children—all of them—safe from harm? The answer is no. We're not doing enough. And we will have to change. —President Barack Obama at the Sandy Hook Prayer Vigil in December 2012.

There were always champions, says Rob, "including now President Joe Biden, but gun safety was, until that point, the third rail of American politics."

Rob saw President Obama's speech, and it moved him quite literally from the couch to his feet. He got as close as he could to the TV, and then tears started flowing down his face. "I was crying, for the children and educators and Sandy Hook, and also for gun violence victims, survivors, and loved ones everywhere. We were being seen."

He thought, *This is it. We will come together, and things will change.* In one breath, he felt both complete sorrow and hope.

But a few days later, National Rifle Association Executive Director Wayne LaPierre gave a public statement and shattered Rob's aspirations for immediate change. For in his statement, LaPierre called for guns in schools. He told the country the only way to protect their children was to bring more guns into their lives.

*It is now time for us to assume responsibility for their
safety at school. The only way to stop a monster from
killing our kids is to be personally involved and invested
in a plan of absolute protection. The only thing that
stops a bad guy with a gun is a good guy with a gun.*
—*Wayne LaPierre in December 2012.*

After watching the familiar news cycle unfold, Rob recalls
thinking to himself, *I have learned some critical skills. I'm
passionate. Maybe the one thing I can contribute to this cause
is my time and effort...my energy. Because that's really the
only thing we can control is what we choose to do with whatever time and effort and energy we have.*

He decided, regardless of how things looked in this
shooting's aftermath, in a country still divided, he would
push on. Just as his aunt and uncle had done after the death
of their daughter. Just as the many volunteers and activists
he had met and witnessed who raised their voices through
their pain.

He picked up the phone and talked to as many gun sense
organizations as he could. He had to find the next best place
where he could work to make a difference. Happily, he landed
right back where he started, at Brady. There, he would learn
how to use his litigation skills to represent survivors of gun
violence and how to hold bad actors across the industry
accountable.

Then he found Everytown for Gun Safety and Moms
Demand Action.

"I saw how much the movement changed from when I
was last doing this kind of national work, before I got my law
degree," Rob said. "Everytown for Gun Safety, and Moms
Demand Action. John Feinblatt and Shannon Watts. I saw

what they were able to accomplish by fighting for policy change, nationally and within the states. They built a movement of grassroots volunteers and survivors and were backed by research and evidence that allowed them to really fight for common sense policies that folks would support."

So, when he got the opportunity to work for Everytown, he jumped. "I just felt like there was so much possibility to do good work," said Rob.

What he didn't expect was that Everytown would ask him to uproot and move to the south where he would be tasked with taking on some very southern gun sense issues.

"All of a sudden I was lobbying in state houses in the southern states. I got to really understand and see the issue in a whole new way," said Rob. "My family owns guns. I grew up with firearms in the house. So, I understood them, and I kind of respected the Second Amendment; but seeing how things worked in some of these southern states, it just gave me a whole new, valuable perspective. Legislators in those states suffer and care just as much as anyone else, but the language is different about guns, so it was about having to find that balance."

That "difference" Rob mentioned refers mostly to a mentality.

"Guns are part of the culture in the south, so the policy solutions have to be tailored to get at the prevention of gun violence while still respecting the rights of responsible, law-abiding citizens," said Rob. "There are loopholes in the laws at every state that could be addressed if the climate was right for action. The problem to be solved was how to find the sweet spot to get something done."

One of Rob's early assignments was to go to Tennessee and work to pass a new gun sense law.

Tennessee was then ranked one of the most conservative state legislatures in the country, but Rob was determined to meet as many people as he could, to cross party lines, and to dredge up issues ripe for change.

Domestic violence, he learned, was one such issue. Legislators across the aisle wanted to work on it.

"Background checks are required on gun sales at all licensed dealers across the country," said Rob. "For most states, those checks are run by the FBI, but some states have opted to have their own state agency run the background check."

Rob learned Tennessee has its own state agency that ran background checks for gun sales and had information on who was denied because they were prohibited. Then, he learned that domestic abusers were failing background checks and that information wasn't going anywhere.

"It was information that was in a database in Nashville rather than in the hands of the local authorities that could intervene and ensure the domestic abuser was not able to access the gun he was trying to purchase from a store," he said. "So, I worked with legislators on a bill."

According to Rob, this bill stated that if a domestic abuser fails a background check, that information should go to the county where that person lives and to the court that issued the original protective order against them.

This way, when a domestic abuser does not pass a background check when attempting to purchase a gun, local law enforcement has the opportunity to intervene, take action, and potentially save a life.

The Tennessean, "Bill toughens law on domestic abusers," *by Kirk A. Bado, June 9, 2016*

Gov. Bill Haslam signed a bill into law Thursday morning that aims to punish those convicted of domestic abuse who attempt to purchase a firearm.

The bill, sponsored by state Sen. Janice Bowling, R-Tullahoma, and state Rep. Karen Camper, D-Memphis, gives more teeth to current laws on illegal purchases of a firearm. The law requires the Tennessee Bureau of Investigation to alert local officials when dangerous individuals—such as domestic abusers facing a final order of protection—fail a background check when attempting to purchase a gun.

"Before, nothing would happen and that's where the story ended," said Kathleen Wright, spokeswoman for the Tennessee chapter of Moms Demand Action for Gun Sense in America. "But now the TBI will be alerted, and they will give that information to law enforcement who will be able to investigate and take it a step further."

Haslam signed the bill along with more than fifty other pieces of legislation in the War Memorial Auditorium on Thursday. Legislators, lobbyists, and advocacy organizations also joined the governor at the event. The bill received widespread bipartisan support this year.

"It's the perfect example of being able to protect people's personal rights in owning a gun, while also keeping people safe," Wright said.

Tennessee has had a deadly history pairing guns and domestic abuse. Between 2006 and 2014, sixty-eight men and 190 women have died in domestic violence-related shootings, according to a study conducted by The Associated Press.

"It is a baby step, but we are so excited that even though Tennessee was voted as the most conservative legislature in the country we are able to find common ground to say 'we believe in the Second Amendment, but there are things that we can do to save lives and promote public safety,'" Wright said.

Advocating for this bill to become law and seeing it come to fruition was his very first gun sense policy success. It also solidified his reasons for dedicating his life to end gun violence and helped his cousin Laura's legacy live on.

"In the House, the bill passed unanimously," Rob said. "I felt so much optimism, but then we got to the Senate and the NRA stepped in. Historically when the NRA got involved and said they opposed a policy, it was the end of the discussion, but this time, a bipartisan group stood up and said, 'This is about domestic abusers in our state who are failing background checks, who are trying to get guns. This is about protecting our mothers, our daughters, our sisters, our friends, and our neighbors.' And I believe we should pass it.'"

No one knew what the outcome would be the next day, but the bill passed twenty-six to four.

"It was a real lesson of how you can build bridges and you can build connections and community by focusing on the issues people care about, and in showing that gun laws can be part of the solution," said Rob.

Today, Rob is the federal legal director at Everytown for Gun Safety.

He has led an effort to stop the NRA's top legislative priority during the Trump era, worked on proactive steps that a gun-sense president in the United States can take to save lives, and spent time with dozens of offices in Washington, DC, on developing effective gun-safety policies that respect the Second Amendment.

But perhaps more important than his day job, he is a true advocate for gun sense laws and for the millions of volunteers and survivors who work alongside him each and every day.

9

LOVE YOU MORE

———

She didn't know what to do other than to love him.
His parents didn't know what to do other than to push him.
And all of them were terrified of what might come next.

By the time my mom Shelley was fifteen years old, she was no stranger to the tolls of drug and alcohol abuse. Her brother, Mike, just thirteen months older than her, was an addict.

Shelley learned quite quickly what it meant to worry not just about grades and boys and everything else that comes with teenage years, but about the mental and physical welfare of the people she loved.

By sixteen years old, her brother Mike quit school all together. His addiction was brewing for more than three years at that point, and it didn't take long for him to drift away from their familial fabric, one already strained by the divorce of their parents six years before.

Shelley's parents were doing the best they could. Her father was a local cop working long, odd hours, and her mother also worked full-time while dealing with the brunt of the emotional drain of drug addiction's toll on her son Mike.

As the eldest child, Shelley quickly grew to feel responsible for her siblings—a single, strong stitch meant to keep the peace between her brother and her family, and to protect her eleven-year-old sister Cindy.

One night, in their small apartment downtown, her mother Paula went to do laundry. She opened the washing machine door, surprised to find a bong and other paraphernalia hidden inside.

Desperate and unsure of what to do about her son, Paula called her ex-husband Carl.

"He's staying out all night. He's hiding drugs in my home. I don't know what to do anymore," she said, sounding defeated.

Carl offered up an option he had learned about through his work as a cop. "I know about this program called Job Corps. It'll keep him busy, hopefully clean him up, and give him a sense of responsibility. We'll get him in immediately."

But, within months of starting the program, Mike passed out under a set of bleachers at a school and was kicked out of the program.

Not quick to give up hope, and increasingly concerned about his Type I diabetes above all else, Paula and Carl set him up at the Josslin Clinic. There, maybe, he would get some better help.

"Nothing ever worked," Shelley recalled. "When he got home, he went straight back to his drugs and drinking."

Shelley didn't know what to do other than to love him. His parents didn't know what to do other than to push him. All of them were terrified of what might come next.

Sometime in 1985, after a long weekend of arguing with Mike over his addiction, Paula came home from work to find a knife stabbed into her mattress.

"It was the last straw," said Shelley. Paula felt unsafe, and that she couldn't submit the family to this anymore. She kicked Mike out of the house that day.

"I was petrified he would kill my mom in her sleep," Shelley said. "My brother was not okay."

Shelley secretly laid out a mattress in the basement so Mike could sneak in and rest. Not knowing where he'd go or how he'd survive, *at least*, she thought, *I could give him this.*

Her secret basement setup became a place where she could make sure he had food, where she could lay eyes on him from time to time, where she could keep watch.

Unaware of Shelley and Mike's basement scheme, Paula dragged on day after day bearing the brunt of her son's absence in her heart.

On Friday nights, after her long work weeks ended, she started to find reprieve from her son's struggles at the bingo hall or the social club down the street where she knew the owners.

Divorced and a mother of three children, with one unraveling at the seams, "Maybe this was just how she coped," Shelley said.

On one of these evenings, Shelley went to the bar where her mother was, picked up cash for a quick meal for her and her sister Cindy, and grabbed the two of them a pizza pie from Maria's Pizza Shop down the block.

"I had just returned with our pizza and went straight down to the basement to make sure to leave some for Mike. I knew he had been down there recently, given the appearance of the mattress where he sometimes slept. I left him a slice, and as soon as I got back upstairs, I heard a knock on the door," said Shelley.

She peeked out of the door slowly to find a man standing there that she didn't know.

"Where is he? Where's Mike?" he said.

"He isn't here. I swear. My mom kicked him out!" Shelley insisted.

"You let him know that he needs to pay up or we are coming back, and we will get the money he owes us from YOU," he threatened.

She shut and locked the door. Thankfully, this man never did return, but she didn't know that then, nor did she have any idea what this would mean for Mike.

Mike's internal pain and struggle manifested into self-harm and destruction for years to come.

At one point, Shelley's uncle took Mike in, attempting to keep him safe and take some strain off his sister Paula. Yet after realizing Mike stole money from him to support his drug habit, he had to let him go.

This pattern continued. More family members made futile attempts. More recovery centers sent him away without success.

Mike would get clean, and Shelley would find hope.

Once, just after I was born, she welcomed him to our home in Errol, New Hampshire. He was clean and seemingly happy. He even researched an AA meeting in a neighboring town in case he'd need it during his stay.

"I was so proud of him," Shelley remembered. "But as always, it did not last long."

A few years after his visit to Errol and in his mid-twenties, Mike married a woman he met at a dance sponsored by a halfway house while he was trying to get clean. Shortly thereafter, he had a son of his own, and he was so excited for his future.

But old habits crept back in, quickly. Before anyone could stop his train of self-inflicted suffering, it landed on his wife.

In a familiar intoxicated spin, Mike held his baby son in a locked room, away from his wife, with a gun in the house. The situation quickly deescalated without intervention, but it did not come without consequence. With the support of Mike's family behind her, his wife left him with their son and never looked back.

Shelley and Paula helped her move out of that house, took his gun, and turned it into the police. Mike soon fell out of touch with everyone, and the family did not hear from him for years.

Shelley decided she couldn't hold onto the thought of what he could be anymore. She had to come to terms with what he was, and what his repeated actions did to herself and her family.

She went to Al-Anon and tried to make sense of how none of her family's efforts ever worked. In these meetings, she came to understand that it was him and only him who could help himself. She had to redirect her focus on healing the trauma she endured as someone who cared for an addict.

She had to let him go.

The last times Shelley saw her brother, he was homeless. First, him asleep on a bench in downtown Beverly, Massachusetts. Next, him leaving a shelter near the dance studio where she'd take me and my sister Amanda each week.

"I had to make the conscious effort to keep Mike away from me and my family. It was very unhealthy for any of us to have him in our lives," Shelley said. She'd been there, and she'd been forced to grow through it. She wouldn't go back.

Her mother Paula was never able to move on.

"Mom and I always had a relationship, but it grew stronger and stronger as the years went on," said Shelley.

Shelley worked through her childhood pains, though they sat heavy in her soul. She even talked through some of her nagging feelings with her mom as an adult...about the way she felt her mom retreated when she needed her most.

"We all needed help back then. We needed you," Shelley told her.

"I did everything I could for you kids at that time," said Paula.

"From my perspective, I felt you were leaving me at home to clean up that mess and be responsible for my sister. I felt there was more you could do," said Shelley.

They agreed to disagree and never spoke of it again, but Shelley was proud of speaking her mind.

She finally felt like she could focus on what was important. Family—her own husband and two daughters—they needed *her* now, and that's where she'd be.

"I forgave my mom," said Shelley. "I came to realize only after having my own children, that my mom did not have a clue then how to deal with what was happening as a single mom who was struggling to make enough money to keep her home and feed her kids. It must have been so hard."

What she didn't realize though, until it was too late, was that Paula was struggling more than she ever let on.

"I think that she took on unnecessary guilt for not being able to help Mike, and it ate her apart," said Shelley.

Mike died at thirty-five years old, a victim of his own demise. Shelley was only able to see the true destruction he had caused her mother after learning of his death.

"She was never the same again," said Shelley. "At fifty-eight years old, she sunk into a deep depression. On the outside she played 'Grammy' for my kids, and she supported me and Cindy as adults. But when she herself got sick a few years later, I think she just gave up."

In July 2012, my Grammy Paula was diagnosed with cancer. We found out that she was quietly living with a tumor on her head for at least ten years. She never said a word, nor did she go to a doctor, until it was just too unbearable to hide.

On November 11 of that same year, less than six months later, she died.

"I think she felt she deserved it somehow. But really, I think she was just ready to go be with her son," said Shelley.

Continuously working through the stages of grief this diagnosis caused her, Shelley is grateful for the many meaningful conversations her and her mother had before she passed.

They came to an understanding about what unfolded between them in their past, made a deeper connection, and resolved a lot of strain—none of which had formed intentionally, all of which a result of shared experience, and a varied level of response and support.

When I was fifteen years-old, the same age Shelley was when she confronted a drug dealer at her door, I was intensely playing the sport of my dreams.

Year-round, Mom drove me to Timbuktu and back. If it meant I was happy and fulfilled as a child, she made it work.

Dead dad aside, how privileged was I?

At fifteen, Shelley's biggest worries should've been about the upcoming school dance or the amazing and terrifying butterflies that come with finding out that your crush would be going.

But drug dealers at your door and addict brothers eating leftover scraps out of your basement? That does stuff to you.

Mom supported herself, and she sought out support when she felt there was not enough around her. She saw her own potential for growth, and she took it. When she had a family of her own, she did everything in her power to make things different.

Ourselves, the people we care about, the people we don't really know but follow on our feeds—big, small, tragic, widespread, undetected. Trauma runs deep. Yet so does growth.

I see it in all the ways my mom worries and cares about me. I also, maybe more importantly, see it when I know she's scared of all the ways life could hurt me, but she tells me to go live it anyway.

Growing up, I took my mom's unwavering support, and the energy that took, for granted because I never knew any different.

If I wanted it, I could achieve it. If I learned right from wrong, I would succeed. If I wanted to do the dang thing, she'd be on the sidelines, in the crowd, or now texting me while I write, with the same, happy, grounded look on her face that says:

I love you more than you'll ever know. You got this.

I'm so proud of Shelley, and I'm so happy to call her mine.

10

CREATING CALM

—

Both began with a slight imbalance.
Each confirmed her distaste for the conventional.

In early April 2019, Marci Zieff opened her front door to find me and her twenty-seven-year-old son Drew, arm-in-arm, giggling about my fractured foot and brand new, ugly orthopedic boot.

With a big smile and a waving hand, she ushered the two of us in. Drew took the lead and I limped close behind.

"Oh dear," Marci said, with genuine concern. "Can I give you Reiki?"

Marci and I met just weeks before at a concert in Boston. Drew was singing lead in his new folk band, Jake Swamp and the Pine.

One month into dating, I wasn't sure about meeting his mom so soon and knew the loud reverberations from the venue's basement speakers wouldn't make it any easier.

But alas, there she was, tall and slender with shoulder-length black hair and strikingly gorgeous eyes.

"Hi! I'm Breezy!" I yelled nervously, trying to make sure she heard me over the noise.

"Nice to meet you! He sounds great, right?" Marci yelled back. Then the music got louder, and more friends and family arrived. We exchanged glances and smiles the rest of the evening, but that was that.

Between the concert and when I thought I would be able to make a better second impression, I fell down an entire flight of stairs at Drew's apartment. And because he and his mom are so close, she was the first person he called.

At her house on that April afternoon, Marci made me feel right at home.

She brought me to her living room where I sat on her leather couch. There, I watched her glide back and forth from the kitchen to grab a towel, a small pillow, and some water for me.

She sat across from me on her coffee table and placed the pillow on her lap. "Put your foot right here," she said, tapping the top of the pillow.

I removed my boot and slowly lifted my bare, severely bruised foot atop her lap.

"Wow," said Marci, softly. "Are you in a lot of pain? How did you fall, exactly? Do you have other injuries?"

I began to recount my story of stepping outside of Drew's second floor bedroom and slipping on the top step in my socks. Diving metaphorically headfirst back into my fall, it took me some time to realize that, while she listened close, she was already performing her energy work.

She hovered her hands just above my black and blues, closed her eyes, and told me she could feel my foot getting warmer.

Reiki.

This alternative Japanese form of medicine was new to me, and I admittedly needed to do a quick Google search to better understand the practice after I left that day, but it's Marci's preferred form of treatment.

I can't confirm whether it expedited my healing process, but I do know in that moment alone with her, I was calm. It was then that we started to bond not just over clumsy falls and our belief in energy and spirits, but also over a shared love for her son, and maybe subconsciously, in both understanding what it means to grow through the things that break us.

Fast forward to the fall of 2020, and Marci sat across from me, virtually on a video call, in a gently lit basement room in her home.

Surrounded by miniature buddha dolls, books on shamanism, a massage table, a salt lamp, and a post-it note from her daughter that reads, *You're amazing + I love yo*u—she was ready to tell me her story.

A story that started long before me and well before Drew.

A tale of two traumas: the first slow and gradual—one that would chart her course, the second sudden and shocking. One that would give her fresh perspective on her purpose.

Both began with a slight imbalance. Each confirmed her distaste for the conventional.

On February 1, 1978, on her sixteenth birthday, Marci walked into the main office of Framingham High School, determined to take her future into her own hands.

"Can I help you with something?" said the office secretary.

"I'd like to drop out," said Marci.

Finally of the age at which it was legal to drop out of high school without her parents' consent, Marci went for it. She was struggling with her ADHD, she didn't fit in, and she was falling behind.

This can't be my only option, she thought. After she signed the paperwork then and there, Marci walked out of school and grabbed the nearest payphone.

"Mom, please come and get me," she said, crying. Her mother came immediately.

Back home with both of her parents, Marci wept, both in relief and fear. "I'm never going back to that school. It feels like jail," she said.

Up to that point, Marci was self-medicating by smoking a lot of pot, skipping school, and failing all her classes.

"It was a really unhappy place for me, and I felt that if I didn't do something drastic, I would be swallowed up and just disappear...I was crying for help but felt like no one was listening," she said.

That was until this day with her parents.

"They listened," said Marci. "My parents were incredibly supportive and caring. They showed me love and understanding."

On the other hand, Marci felt judged by school and community members for being a "bad kid...and a failure," she said.

"I lost most of my friends and my babysitting jobs. It was a painful time for me and my family, but we stuck together," said Marci.

Yet one day, not long after she left school, her guidance counselor showed up at her front door.

"Hi Marci, can I come in? I have an idea, and I'd love to show you," they said.

While she felt like everyone from school was avoiding her, this one person sought her out and showed her a simple act of kindness that would forever impact her life.

Seated together on their cozy family sectional, Marci's guidance counselor handed her a pamphlet that read *Sudbury Valley School*.

"It's an alternative school, with very different and unstructured methods of learning," they told her.

This opportunity sat outside of the norm, which was exactly where Marci wanted to be.

Though skeptical, still feeling traumatized by her public school experience, Marci agreed. She wanted another chance to care about her education.

Fewer than six months later and just two weeks into being a new student at Sudbury Valley School, Marci had friends, freedom, and a renewed sense of self-confidence.

She was showed kindness, humor, and above all else, support. She made her own schedule, played four square when she wanted a break, took walks in the woods, and often asked staff member Marge to teach her and her friends how to cook—all during school hours.

"There was something magical about having the freedom to explore our own interests. We were not graded or judged. I felt like I could breathe," said Marci.

Marci excelled.

In this setting, she learned it wasn't school she hated; it was the structured environment and the way it hindered her otherworldly tendencies. In fact, she loved to learn, and when allowed to be herself, quickly made friends.

After just two years, she received her high school diploma on time.

Deciding then that she was better equipped to manage additional schooling and that this time she'd approach it in her own way no matter what, she jumped back into the traditional school system and pursued a degree in human services from the University of Massachusetts. In 1985, she graduated with honors.

Ten years later, Marci was introduced to shamanism— the ancient healing wisdom of indigenous people, and a unique connection to spirit and nature rather than intellect (creating-calm.com, 2021).

This introduction served as one of many steps on her continued path down alternative and unconventional growth and healing.

"I also started taekwondo and loved it," Marci said. "I wanted to become a black belt but was really anxious, so I looked at holistic healing practices to help me and soon found meditation."

Meditation did the trick. Marci worked day and night to earn not only her first-degree black belt, but also her second-degree black belt as well.

"All of it helped me focus and stay calm in situations where I wasn't able to in the past. Friends and family started to notice a positive difference in me and the way I related to the world. I knew I wanted to share what I had learned to help others," she said.

So, in 2007, Marci opened her own business, Creating Calm.

"At first, my focus was on helping children to learn calming tools," she said. "I felt like if we taught these tools to children there would be less suffering, less anxiety, and more hope and love. Over time this grew to their families and other adults navigating all sorts of transitions, trauma, illness, anxiety, grief."

But just as the practice started to pick up, Marci's focus would need to circle back on herself.

In 2009, at forty-seven years old, Marci walked into Emerson Hospital for a routine mammogram.

To her surprise, while she awaited the "all clear," Marci was called back into the office.

"We'd like to take another image," said the nurse. After the second round of pushing, prodding, and squishing of her bare breasts between two cold pieces of machinery, Marci was ushered by a radiologist into their office to read the results.

Pointing at a scan of her chest, the radiologist narrowed in on one particular spot. "There's something here we want to take a closer look at. Let's do a biopsy," they said.

Marci made it out to her car, but how she got there was a blur.

"I was in shock," she said. "I called my husband who was at work and didn't pick up. I didn't want to call my mother because she had her own experience with breast cancer, and I wasn't ready to worry her."

So Marci sat in her car, alone and scared, and decided to call a friend. Her friend answered and together they cried.

Not long after Marci got home, her friend was by her side, helping to research doctors and map out next steps.

"I was told my results would take about a week after my biopsy was done." said Marci. "But my phone rang less than twenty-four hours after the procedure."

Alone again, she picked up.

"You have something called ductal carcinoma in situ," said the doctor on the other end of the phone. Having DCIS, as Marci would soon learn, meant the cells that line the milk ducts of her breast had become cancerous.

Once she hung up, she couldn't think.

"Our dog, Ollie, needed to go out. My brain was in a fog. I took Ollie for a walk, not ready to call my family," she said. She called the same friend who had helped her the day of the mammogram.

How am I going to tell my family? Marci thought. *What do I say?*

She put on a brave face and told her children what the doctors told her.

"The cancer hasn't spread to any surrounding tissue. They told me that of the different types of breast cancer someone can have, this is a best case scenario," she said.

She put the business on hold and agreed to radiation. Before she knew it, she was at the hospital every single day for treatment.

"It was painful and went on for six weeks," said Marci.

But just before finishing radiation, Marci learned about a local, holistic business called Roots and Wings Healing Arts that had office space available for rent.

"One thing cancer taught me was to go after the things important to me and to not wait for the perfect moment," she said.

The day before her final radiation appointment, Marci went to visit the space. She signed the lease that day.

"It felt like a huge triumph," said Marci. "A new beginning and a way of saying to myself that cancer was not going to stop me from moving forward and reaching my goals."

Even while enduring two lumpectomies and radiation, above all else, she moved forward.

"I was always interested in Reiki and went for a session about six months after finishing radiation," said Marci. "It offered me renewed calm and balance, so when the practitioner offered a certification, I joined and became a certified Reiki practitioner in 2010."

Marci has since completed the highest level of Reiki certifications and was named a Reiki master of masters, offering both private Reiki treatments and group certifications.

Two years after her first diagnosis and cleared from further treatment, Marci walked into her doctor's office for her annual mammogram.

There, unprepared, she was hit with diagnosis two.

Her practice was finally back up and running. She felt energized, centered, and ready to expand the business. Yet, once again, Marci found herself getting another biopsy, and awaiting the dreaded phone call.

In less than twenty-four hours, her phone rang, and this time with her husband right next to her, she learned she had breast cancer on the opposite side.

This is going to be different, Marci thought.

She would take control and maybe, by following her intuition, she'd never have to go through anything like this again. Not long after, she was scheduled for her self-elected double mastectomy.

The months that followed her surgery were filled with infections, allergic reactions, countless medications, and complete reconstructive surgery. As part of a school project, Marci's daughter Sara wrote about the experience:

> *She was in and out of the hospital, and I was terrified of losing my mom…I had issues paying attention in school and often left in tears to visit her. Every day, I waited for a call that she would be rushed into surgery. When she was finally home for good, she could not do a lot for herself. I could tell she was miserable and tired of feeling dependent on others.*

But when I asked Marci about what she remembers from this time, she didn't want to focus on the pain as much as she wanted to talk about Sara's school play.

Because just after her surgery, extremely sore and wearing a large button-down shirt to hide her surgical drains, Marci picked up where she left off.

"I wasn't going to miss her in *Legally Blonde*," Marci told me. She also jumped right back into growing her business.

"My personal experience with cancer has helped me to be a better healer for my clients," she said. "They are comforted by my understanding of what it's like to get this diagnosis and go through treatment. I can provide support and holistic healing for countless others on their journey through illness. For that, I'm very grateful."

Now more than eight years cancer free, and having undergone intense conventional treatments, Marci has found health, happiness, and continued growth in the art of healing others, unconventionally.

"It's amazing to see the way Reiki, energy work, shamanic practices, and meditation shifts and impacts lasting change on so many levels—emotionally, spiritually, and physically," said Marci.

"I used all of these holistic healing practices to help me release the fear and sadness that came with a cancer diagnosis. It's really special to be able to offer this experience to others."

Though life changing, Marci only sees cancer as a part of her story.

"It is not who I am," she said.

As a matter of fact, when you ask her what she's most proud of, defeating cancer doesn't even make the list.

"I'm most proud of my family and the closeness we share," said Marci. "I'm proud of doing my best to be a great mother, wife, sister, daughter, and friend. I'm proud of building a business I love and helping others navigate their challenges with a new perspective."

She also lights up when talking about her second-degree black belt in taekwondo. "Receiving my black belt felt unattainable, but the process and my triumphs taught me so many lessons about myself, perseverance, self-confidence, integrity, and courage," she said.

Marci came into my life unexpectedly and untraditionally, which I find very fitting.

While picking up the pieces of my once picture-perfect life, crushed by the reality that not everyone finds love, gets married, has a baby, and lives happily ever after, I fell head over heels for her son Drew.

It wasn't conventional, and I will admit it was fast. I moved out on my own for the first time in eight years with a baby and divorce papers in tow, and decided I was too young and too full of life to disallow myself to live it.

I started to spend time with Drew, and for the first time in a year, I had hope. No matter where it led me or us, my gut was telling me that with him, in this moment, I could relax, and that's all I needed.

It was a bonus that he came with a family, and especially with Marci, who welcomed me and my daughter with glee.

In the two and a half years I've spent around Marci, she has demonstrated to me the importance of learning to trust oneself, of leaning into intuition, and that no matter the choice—education or health or relationship—she believes it is ours to make.

11

330 DAYS

———

Growth is no tsunami.
It doesn't just happen.
It rolls through in gentle waves,
sometimes so quietly that it goes unnoticed,
until and unless we make the time to see it.

At 10 p.m. on the night of January 14, 2019, Eliza Valori finished watching *The Bachelor* alone in the living room of her two-bedroom apartment in Hershey, Pennsylvania.

She shut off the TV and made sure all the doors were locked. Then she walked upstairs and just before entering her own room, she noticed her roommate's door was open.

Her roommate was inside, and she had fallen asleep.

At 11:30 p.m., Eliza heard footsteps crunching in the snow outside her window. Confused, she held her breath to listen. She heard a gate unlatch and a sliding door open and close.

She assumed the commotion was coming from a neighbor's house. She did live in an apartment complex after all, and dogs barked in the distance. *Maybe they were just letting them out to pee*, she thought.

But all of a sudden, she heard something downstairs—coming from inside her home.

Eliza got up and looked out her window above the back door, but it was too dark to see anything. She turned on the flashlight on her phone, but that just obstructed her view when it reflected off the glass in front of her.

She knew something was wrong, and her senses started firing.

She quickly got back in bed, scared. There it was again. Her sliding door opened and closed.

Then heavy footsteps started marching up the stairs leading to her bedroom.

Eliza, who is a hundred pounds soaking wet, is petite, gentle, and kind. The man who barged into her room moments later could not have been more opposite of her.

Eliza quickly realized this was not her roommate. This was a large, intimidating person she did not know. She screamed bloody murder and hoped and prayed someone—her roommate, her neighbors, anyone—would hear her.

"Who are you? What is your name? Why are you here? What is going on?" Eliza yelled.

"Shut up, you dumb bitch! Be quiet. The neighbors are going to hear," he said back, and then he charged toward her.

She realized he was holding a knife in his right hand and wearing white rubber gloves. He had a flashlight in his left hand and shined it on her, revealing the much smaller person he had in front of him. He wore all black and had the hood of his sweatshirt covering his head and a multicolored scarf over his face.

"Please don't hurt me. I want to live!" she cried.

"Get on your stomach," he said.

"No! I have a mother, a father, a brother. I'm a nurse at the children's hospital," she said pointing desperately out her window and across the street.

He covered her mouth and told her to shut up. He pointed his knife at her. Eliza grabbed the inside of his wrist to push it away from her body.

"Don't be brave. Don't be a hero. Do as I say or else you'll get hurt," he said.

Eliza tried to say something but was hit hard across her right cheek. In the dark and chaos, she didn't know exactly what happened but assumed he struck her with his flashlight.

Just do what he says, she thought to herself. *This is how it's going to be.*

"I'm not here to kill you. I'm here to rob you. Get on your stomach," he said. She didn't believe him. She thought she was going to be raped.

"Where is my money?" he said, louder and in her face.

"What? Do you know who I am? I don't think you have the right house!" said Eliza, confused. She never carried cash, and she couldn't think of much to offer him.

"If you'll let me up, I'll get you my wallet. I only carry plastic. Let me show you," she pleaded.

"No fun and games," he said and backed away from her. Eliza walked over to her work bag and quickly opened her wallet to show him nothing was there.

"Here! Take my cards, anything," she said. He rummaged through it and even glanced at her driver's license. "Is your name Eliza?" He dumped the change he found in his sweatpants pocket. "What's your PIN number?" he asked.

She paused but decided to give in and tell him. "You're lying. You hesitated. I have someone downstairs. We will go to the ATM and if you're wrong, you will get hurt," he said.

Then they were both startled by a door slamming shut.

"Who's there?" Eliza yelled. No response.

"Get back on your bed and face the wall," he told her.

"No, you still have a knife," she said. "I need to see what you're doing. Please. I don't trust you won't hurt me. You're scaring me."

Eliza got back in bed but positioned herself so she could still see him.

She saw flashlights outside, and they seemed to be pointed at her room. Moments later, she heard pounding on her front door.

"52 Townhouse open up! It's the police," a welcomed voice yelled.

Her roommate, who was asleep across the hall when the intruder broke in, had heard the commotion and immediately called 911. The dispatcher instructed her to close her bedroom door, lock it, and hide in her closet until the police arrived.

"Shut up. Don't say a word or else you'll get hurt," the intruder whispered to Eliza.

The banging continued, louder this time. He glanced out the window, noticed something, and then bolted out of her room, down the stairs, and straight out the front door.

Numb.

She was completely—physically and emotionally—numb.

She didn't know if it was over, or if her roommate was okay, or if the police were there, or if her intruder was gone for good.

After a few minutes, she came to and ran to her roommate's room. She tapped on the door. "It's me, Eliza," she said.

Nothing.

She peered over the top of the stairs.

Finally, she saw a police officer and immediately burst into tears. "I was just held up at knifepoint in my bedroom!" she told him, while beginning to hyperventilate. "I can't breathe," she said and fell to the floor.

Her roommate then came out of her room and hugged her.

Escorted downstairs by the police officer, Eliza noticed her TV was missing. *He must have came in and out twice,* she thought. *He didn't bring the TV to my bedroom.*

The police told them their intruder was subdued in the parking lot and was taken into custody. They tracked his footprints in the snow and found their TV, DVD player, and DVDs in the backseat of his car in the lot behind their house.

By the time they were done taking their statements and acquiring evidence, it was 3 a.m. on January 15, but Eliza did not feel safe.

She refused to stay there.

Eliza texted some of her coworkers to see if anyone was awake and was quickly offered a place to sleep by a couple of the nurses. Eliza and her roommate quickly packed overnight bags and drove to one of her coworker's houses.

Neither slept, and the two decided to return home at 6:30 a.m. to warn the neighbors about what happened. To their surprise, no one heard a thing, nor did they yet know about the break-in.

By 8 a.m. that morning, the press got wind of the crime and reported that the victims worked for the local hospital.

Eliza's manager reached out and said the PR team was handling the influx of media inquiries and would not provide their names. So, Eliza requested some time off.

Maybe I'll just take a couple of shifts off and get my head straight, she thought.

Just a bit later that morning, her phone rang again. This time, it was a detective who wanted to meet in person. Although the intruder was already in custody, they said they needed a recorded statement and to corroborate Eliza's account with her roommate's.

At 1 p.m. that day, Eliza and her roommate entered the police station for this meeting.

Eliza offered to go first and was escorted into a small conference room where two detectives and a victim advocate sat together at a table.

She was barraged with questions.

Nervous, still in shock, and trying to give an accurate account of what happened, she was interrupted repeatedly by one of the detectives.

"And then what happened?" they asked. "Where are you from? How long have you lived in Hershey? Where do you work? What is your boyfriend's name and where does he live? What did you do all day yesterday?"

She knew they were trying to help and figure out why this man chose their house to enter that night, but she was tired and overwhelmed. Content that the perpetrator was in custody and that she'd get justice, she didn't ask them any questions and insisted she was ready to leave.

Though Eliza didn't want to go home. *I can't live in that apartment for one more second*, she thought.

When she got back from that meeting, she packed a duffel bag, unsure of how long she'd be gone, and left as soon as she could. She drove straight to her aunt and uncle's house in Monkton, Maryland, about an hour and a half away.

Before the attack, twenty-seven-year-old Eliza was an average, fresh-faced nursing student.

In May 2018, just seven months earlier, she graduated from an accelerated nursing program, passed her boards, landed her very first job, and moved from her school apartment in Philadelphia to her new home in Hershey, Pennsylvania.

She was in a long-term relationship with her then-boyfriend of six years, with hopes of soon getting married and moving in with one another. In the meantime, she was getting used to her new schedule, job, and living situation.

Yet she wouldn't have much time for any of it.

In the afternoon hours the day after her attack, Eliza arrived at her aunt and uncle's house and was immediately surrounded with love, comfort, and safety. They encouraged her to stay as long as she needed, but that just wasn't Eliza's way.

No, she thought. *Don't be a burden.* She would figure out how to brush this off and push past her fears.

Three days later, she returned to Hershey with every intention of working her Saturday shift.

When she got home, she couldn't bear the eerie feeling she got once she stepped inside.

Her body was fighting every step she took toward her room, and when she opened her bedroom door, the over-the-door towel rack made the same exact clanking sound it did on the night of her attack.

Just like that, she screamed and was right back in the thick of it.

Once again, she felt she had to escape but she didn't know where to go. That night, she slept with her roommate. *At least it isn't my own bed*, she thought, *where everything happened.*

Eliza never actually slept.

"That was the second worst night of my life. I stared at her bedroom door waiting for someone to come barging in," she said. "I was afraid to close my eyes, and when I finally drifted off to sleep, I woke up soon after, screaming and drenched in sweat."

It was then that she started to admit to herself she needed help. She requested additional time off from work and started to research support.

By chance, her primary care doctor just happened to call days after the incident for a follow up to a routine visit. She told them what happened and how she was struggling to cope.

Her doctor brought her in for a visit with a social worker. They checked on her mental and physical wellbeing, sent her for facial X-rays to check on her injury from the night of the break-in, and prescribed her something to help her sleep.

Eliza wanted to work on sleeping without medication, but she was comfortable knowing she could fill the prescription and have it there if need be.

Her father came to town two weeks later to be with her for the first court hearing, but at the last minute, the hearing was canceled. They decided to follow through with their plans to stay together and spent that night in a local hotel in separate rooms.

Near the elevator, Eliza's room let in every sound from the foot traffic nearby. She found the experience excruciating. She was in a constant state of panic, hadn't slept in days, and made a middle-of-the-night attempt with the concierge to request a different room.

I can't do this anymore, she thought, and promised her dad before he left she'd stay with her aunt and uncle until she found a place of her own that made her comfortable. She would also start taking the medication her doctor prescribed.

Just over two weeks after the attack, Eliza and her roommate moved back in together in a new apartment ten minutes away.

They installed a security system and added a dead-bolt lock on the front door. Her roommate's dad even gave them a custom slab of wood to fit in the groove of their sliding door. Ultimately, though, none of it mattered. Eliza still feared for her life.

One month after the incident, the pre-trial hearing started.

Eliza entered the courtroom from the back and immediately saw her attacker standing there in an orange jumpsuit. He turned to look at her in the doorway and she froze. He was seeing her in the light of day, and her, him.

She couldn't take it.

Eliza started crying, shaking, and frantically looked for a place to sit far from his view. A court officer and victim advocate escorted her to a seat, and she sat, freezing and uncontrollably scared.

It doesn't matter what I do, she thought. *I'll never feel safe.*

She moved out of the home where the attack happened, her intruder was in jail, she found a new, safe neighborhood and installed every type of system they could imagine, but she still found herself in a constant need to run.

"I took every opportunity to leave the area. I spent many weekends with my boyfriend in Maryland, and when he was working, I would just stay with his dad in New Jersey," she said.

All she knew was that she couldn't be anywhere near where it happened, and she most certainly couldn't be alone.

The most immediate effects of her trauma were obvious.

A complete inability to sleep. No appetite. One hundred percent irritability. Every movement and every noise sent her anxiety skyrocketing. Bright lights, footsteps, and doors triggered her memories of that night, and it made her terrified of adjusting to new surroundings.

The unexpected was always the worst.

Her constant and saving grace became the church community she found while she was in nursing school. Her boyfriend's family lived twenty-five minutes away in Mantua, New Jersey, and introduced her to the congregation.

"My faith was strengthened from enduring this trauma. It has been a huge pillar in my recovery," said Eliza.

Sometimes, she returns to Mantua to stay with her now-husband's family and together they visit the church. The pastors and community check in with her and pray over her, and her friends from bible study do the same.

"Recovering from trauma is not linear; it has been more of a rollercoaster. Hearing how far I have come from their point of view is eye opening," said Eliza. "I am always hard on myself, so to hear how amazed they are at my progress or point out things I have pushed myself to accomplish helps me feel empowered."

She also started talk therapy following her attack. With her therapist's help, Eliza does a lot of work reframing experiences and environments that trigger her flight response.

It has been over two years since the incident, yet Eliza is still waiting for justice to be served.

"I look forward to the day that I am able to testify in court," said Eliza. "This ordeal will not be over for me until he is sentenced, and I am given the opportunity to read a victim impact statement. He may never fully comprehend what he did to me that night, but I hope he hears the pain and despair he caused."

During this turmoil, Eliza and her boyfriend got married and moved in together. Since, she hasn't often found herself alone, but she's recognized that when she has, her instinct is no longer to flee.

"At this point in my recovery, I realize if I continue with avoidance, it will only get harder. It wasn't an easy feat, but each night I spend alone, I make progress," she said.

The first time her husband traveled overnight for work, Eliza tried to sleep in the living room with every light on and slept for maybe three hours total. The following night, she moved to the bedroom and slept one more hour than the last.

On New Year's Eve 2019, 330 days after her attack, Eliza celebrated a full night's sleep.

She shared the following post on her Instagram profile with a photo of herself smiling in a field of sunflowers:

It took 330 days to be able to fall asleep without the notion that my life would be in danger in the middle of the night again. It goes without saying that this year has been the hardest year of my life. A year ago, I was excited for everything that was falling into place in my life. Never in my wildest dreams could I have envisioned the trauma I would be faced with fourteen days into the new year.

It took me a long time to believe in myself again, but I am confident saying that I am a Survivor, an Overcomer. My struggle isn't over yet and I'm ready for justice to be served. 2019 tested my faith and strengthened it all the while. You can't do life alone, and there are so many individuals I'm thankful for, those who encouraged me, reached out to me, welcomed me back to work with so much love and support, prayed for me at all hours of the day and night, and loved me as I transformed into a different version of myself as I processed the events of that night and began my healing and recovery.

I hold my head a little bit higher and raise my voice a little bit louder now. I am brave, courageous, and fearless. I may have felt like I had no choice in the moment to have those qualities but looking back I now realize I was equipped to fight. I found a strength I've never known. I firmly believe He was standing in my room that night, right beside me, protecting me and assisting me until help arrived.

I pray for deep healing in 2020, to move forward with peace and clarity; to be still and know that in the waiting, God is fighting for me and preparing my testimony in court to be victorious. I will be patient and have faith that in 2020 that day will come

Since her attack, Eliza also battled newfound self-doubt and continues to work on the ways in which she shows herself love.

I'm not good enough. I can't do anything right. These thoughts fill her mind more often than she'd like to admit, but she's decided to be mindful of it and to redirect the negativity.

She knows growth is no tsunami. It doesn't just happen. It rolls through in gentle waves, sometimes so quietly it goes unnoticed, until and unless we make the time to see it.

"I've used a lot of reflection to identify what is triggering me and how it could be linked to what I have gone through," she said. "Retelling this story still takes my breath away."

Though she can't rid these memories entirely, she's learning how to see them for what they are and to put them where *she* wants. She's focusing instead on what's next.

"I want to move forward with my life. I want a family, to raise children in the suburbs…to go back to school to become a pediatric nurse practitioner, travel the world, and be an advocate for others," she said.

I can see her doing just that.

I met Eliza as we entered high school. Both awkward and shy, I was comforted by her soft demeanor and squeaky, contagious giggle. She didn't care if I was as cool as I strived to be; she just wanted to be my friend. Until writing this, I realize, I never thanked her for that.

When I royally screwed up my teenage years by igniting the fire that became my high school experience—Eliza was there. She didn't give up on me, and she wholeheartedly cared if I was okay.

After high school, she moved out of state while I stayed put. We went to separate colleges, made new friends, and as with many high school relationships, we lost touch.

Scrolling through Facebook in October of 2019, I saw an obscure post she made about never knowing what others are going through:

Apparently, it's World Mental Health Day, and as this day comes to a close, I would just like to remind everyone to be kind. You have no idea what another is struggling with.

Someone stated to my peer that I "don't smile enough." That statement has echoed in my head for months now. I desperately wanted to scream at her, "You have no idea what I have been through in the last six months. How dare you—you barely know me!" But I didn't because I don't owe her anything; I didn't have to justify my emotions to her, or anyone.

It's okay to not be okay. It's okay to ask for help. Be kind, it's not rocket science, it's basic human decency.

We hadn't talked in years. *Do I reach out? Is it weird after all this time to ask her if she's okay?*

I should have, because in hindsight, I know she wasn't but that shouldn't have mattered either way.

When I was workshopping this book, her posts popped into my head, and when I reached out to her, she answered me with the same welcoming response I would have always expected from her. She was eager to schedule a video date and to catch up, and she was willing to share her story.

Eliza is a walking, lifesaving, badass pillar of strength, resilience, and growth. I am so inspired by her story—one that until this moment remained publicly untold.

I will forever carry with me the lessons I've gleaned from her about compassion, openness, and understanding—about friendship and what it really means to offer and be offered support.

12

BETTER YET

———

More importantly,
I heard about all the ways people grew from that.
How they grew through that.
Better yet, how they used that, for good.

One day, while writing this book, my mom handed me a thick black binder.

There was a photo of my dad and a prayer card from his funeral on the front, and its contents were bursting at the seams.

Mom was in possession of this binder long before I ever craved its existence—a time capsule from the year Dad died.

It had hospital bills and lawyers' correspondences, even letters from the man who killed him. Photos, cards, flyers, and newspaper clippings. Now, in my hands, lay every gruesome detail I ever wanted to know, stitched up with laminate, a three-hole punch, and there on top, my dad's smiling face.

I spent three quiet afternoon hours alone, wiping tears from my eyes, peeling through its pages.

Pay up, wrote the bill collectors.

The front of Mom's binder she made the year Dad died.

Detailed hospital bills explained everything they did to my dad when he was rolled in that day, and apparently, trying to save his life wasn't cheap.

Tell us more, wrote the lawyers.

Mounds of letters back and forth between my mom and the law office created a yearlong timeline to show how they pieced my family's life together so they could come up with a number equivalent to my father's worth.

Good family, sad times, wrote the newspapers.

Small-town publications called Mom repeatedly, each vying to be the first to cover the latest in the DiPietro family tragedy.

Though she tucked these pages neatly in a row, color-coded and labeled, it was clear to me she found comfort in making sense of this chaos.

Between working full-time, selling Dad's business, attending lawyers' meetings and court proceedings with her new baby perched high on her hip, and dealing with finances and the media, Mom made the most time for us.

She took us to therapy, gymnastics meets, dance class, and grocery shopping. She advocated for a fair and just sentence for the man who murdered our father. She worked with lawyers to ensure we received a settlement that would help us survive. And she made sure we continued to grow through counseling, healthy activity, and the support of a community we loved.

As I closed this binder, I realized that not only was I in awe of her strength and the way she worked through the repeated traumas that unfolded after Dad's death, but was also struck by the way we were engulfed with love.

Humility and kindness didn't just come from those we would always have expected to be there, but also from neighbors, colleagues, and community members who saw what we were going through and thought, *I'll be there, whatever it takes.*

This is what continues to pull at my heart strings the most: the action, the people, and my mom's strength. It isn't every gritty detail that I thought I longed for all those years, but the support and care I now know we received during our most intense time of need.

It is the way all of it helped us bear the weight of the trauma.

According to a 2021 Pew Research Center survey, roughly half of Americans (53 percent) favor gun sense laws and the same amount (48 percent) see gun violence as a very big problem in this country.

That also means, though, that half of my fellow citizens don't favor gun sense laws, nor do they see it as an issue worth fighting for.

The same can be said for my family.

Throughout this book, I've talked about my people, and I've shared a lot about my immediate family. Now is as good a time as any to mention my extended family and our polarities.

Because when it comes to gun sense issues, we do not all feel the same.

Though they also lost my dad on that June day—some of them still believe in, and advocate for, the right to own a gun.

They have them, they love them, and they fully support the National Rifle Association.

Though it pains me to say it, my dad loved guns too. Yet I've recently come to learn this shouldn't be surprising, because a staggering one third of all US adults own a gun (Gallup, 2020).

My dad supported the NRA, enjoyed hunting, and owned a couple of guns himself. He grew up in a gun-toting family, and he was raised to believe each and every one of us has the big, brave, and bold American right to use them.

My family and I share the same blood, but never the same opinion.

This is exactly why Everytown for Gun Safety, Moms Demand Action, and other like-minded organizations focus their efforts not on control or the removal of guns all together, but on the root causes, by bringing to the surface the many positive and feasible ways we can save lives together, no matter what you believe in.

Gun sense is a nonpartisan issue that can only be solved by removing party lines, by shaking hands on common ground and focusing on key areas of interest.

This includes responsible gun ownership and safety, strengthening background checks, gun education in schools, removing senseless loopholes that allow dangerous people and repeat offenders to get their hands on guns, and more.

These issues affect all our lives in one way or another, and are just as important as talking about and working on the end results we see all too often: mass shootings, homicide, domestic abuse, suicide, and accidental shootings.

Because of the way my traumas shaped me, I have trouble understanding how anyone could feel the pain and consequence of gun violence and still believe in the need for the Second Amendment...nor do I want to exert too much energy trying to understand how they could support the violent rhetoric of the NRA.

Instead, I'll listen to Shannon Watts, Greg Gibson, and every survivor and volunteer I've met or followed along the way who teach me that to create positive change in the gun sense movement is to find effective, collaborative ways to blur party lines, to focus on the why, and to put it simply, to save lives.

I'd love to believe my dad's views would have evolved over time, or that together, we would have come to understand one another's beliefs. I want to believe he would have listened to me and respected me if I wanted to fight for change. But as much as I like to speculate, he's gone, and I must face my facts:

My dad was killed by an irresponsible act of gun violence, and I'm here, writing this book, because of it.

One year after my dad's death, Mom sent a letter to the editors of our local newspapers to thank the community at large for the role they played in our family's survival.

Because though she and our family had spent a year grieving such an immense loss, we also witnessed the true meaning of community.

> *Our dreams of a full, stable family were just starting to become a reality, until June 17, 1997 when a single gunshot shattered our dreams forever.*
>
> *That is the day my husband died, leaving behind a wife, two beautiful daughters, and a son who was still three months from birth. It was the worst day of my life.*
>
> *What would I do without him? He was my everything.*

Those who knew my late husband knew of his great personality, warmth, charm, and sense of humor. Those of you whom I speak of are missing him as much as I am.

As the anniversary of his death approaches, I wanted to express my gratitude for all the wonderful people in our lives who have helped us through a horrible year. Without your strength and support, I am not quite sure how I would have survived and gone on to be the strength that my children so desperately needed.

I am sure Bob would want me to thank you for taking such good care of us. He truly loved me and his children with all of his heart. (DiPietro, 1998)

With the lessons I've learned, and my mother's humbled, gracious sentiment in mind, I'm redirecting my energy toward what matters most: my passion, my people, and what comes next.

I took a leap of faith when I decided to write this book—not because I felt what I had to say was wrong or I wouldn't be able to do it, but because I had no set structure for what exactly I was hoping to share.

I only knew I had a relentless desire to share it.

My dad died at the age of thirty, and I was about to turn thirty myself.

When I told my boyfriend Drew about this idea, he asked me, "What type of advice or stories do you wish you could hear from your dad as you turn thirty?"

That's it! I thought. *My book will be about the age and about finding myself, learning from the past, and hearing from others what I wish I could hear from my dad.*

Hell, I too had some life to share. I lost my father to gun violence. I dealt with an eating disorder. I was engaged at twenty-four, married at twenty-five, a mom at twenty-six, and divorced at twenty-seven.

I set out, without too much more thought, and before I knew it, I was interviewing a handful of people who had some pretty great wisdom to share.

But something became abundantly and quickly clear: It wasn't clicking.

My heart didn't care about thirty, the age. It cared about thirty, *his final age*, and I was about to be the same.

I paused and thought, *Maybe I could explore gun sense, not as a topic, but a motivator...an inspiring theme.*

I circled my way right back to what I'm most passionate about and what I wish I could spend every minute of every day fighting for. Yet I wrestled with how to do it.

I didn't want to write a book solely focused on the acts of gun violence and the work left to be done. I wanted to figure out a new way in: a written piece of art, of me, and of others, that would yes, raise awareness of the need to end gun violence, but would also shine a light on the potential for what's possible when we harness our pain.

I heard countless stories of challenges and struggle, of life and loss and missteps. But more importantly, I heard about all the ways people grew from that. How they grew through that.

Better yet, how they used that for good.

Growth. There it is.

This book will be about the ways people grow from trauma, big and small, and the potential for what's possible when we do.

I decided to do my best to honor my dad's life and death in the process and to amplify the work millions are doing to stop other people suffering a familiar fate.

Me, my brother Nick (center) and sister Amanda (right) at a memorial bench for our dad in Bartlett, NH.

Bad things happen—to us and because of us. We are human and that is life, but I believe some things, of varying consequence, are traumatic and TRAUMATIC. They warp our vision of ourselves and our surroundings.

Sometimes, and maybe more often than we realize, we allow that vision to become our reality. A living, breathing portrait in our mind that sways our decisions, makes us fearful, timid, or anxious. A constant reminder that life is terrifying.

I also believe our portraits are never fully finished.

We don't have to stare at the same dumpster fire of a picture in our minds forever. We can study it, talk about it, and learn from it. We can be motivated by it to do better for ourselves, for others, or even in honor of others.

Then, we can do what we want with it. Keep it there as a reminder if that's going to help us grow. Or grab a brush and a new, shiny can of paint and go to town. Take control of it and make it ours.

I wish I could talk to my dad about this. I'd want to hear all his stories and learn about his growth. I'd want his advice, from him in his fifties to me now thirty.

I'll never know what he would have told me, so I asked it of everyone else.

WHAT WOULD YOU TELL YOUR YOUNGER SELF IF YOU EVER GOT THE CHANCE?

"You are braver than you feel. The world is scary, but you don't have to always be scared. Everyone else is struggling and just as uncomfortable as you are in their own way. Trust your gut. And of course, choose happy."

AMANDA WAIT, AGE THIRTY-THREE

"Be gentle with yourself; you're doing the best you can."

ELIZA VALORI, AGE TWENTY-NINE

"Do you have any idea who you are? What are you so afraid of?"

GREG GIBSON, AGE SEVENTY-FIVE

"Love yourself more."

LEONA FORMAN, AGE EIGHTY

"Show love and kindness to yourself first. Try not to compare yourself to others. You're the only you. Don't sweat the small stuff."

MARCI ZIEFF, AGE FIFTY-EIGHT

"Keep loving people. Find a way to harness and distill the things you read and learn. Make something out of it. Write in your journal more. Tell more stories. Sell something."

MIKE AMBASSADOR BRUNY, AGE FORTY-THREE

"The journey will be long, so make sure that you learn something new at each step that will help in the future. After twenty years you'll be fortunate to have the friends, family, colleagues, skills, and experiences to be a difference maker."

ROB WILCOX, AGE FORTY

"Don't be afraid to fail. If I let the fear of not knowing everything stop me, I probably still would not have created Moms Demand Action all these years later."

SHANNON WATTS, AGE FIFTY

"Be flexible. Readjust. It's not always going to go to plan, whatever that plan may be. Sometimes it's a better path you end up on. Hang on tight to your heart, your family, and your friends, because you're going to need them more than you know."

SHELLEY MULLARKEY, AGE FIFTY-ONE

"Life will happen, good and bad. Don't force it. Don't stress over it. Just live it."

LOVE, ME, AGE THIRTY

Me with my daughter in fall 2020. Photo credit: Rebecca Leach / Rebecca Rose Photography

RESOURCES

——

I discovered Shannon Watts, Moms Demand Action, and Everytown for Gun Safety when I was searching for a place to put my pain.

Ever since, I've committed to giving what I can to support their efforts: purchasing merchandise and sending donations, amplifying key messages, successes, and campaigns across my social media platforms, and signing up for events to share my story, volunteer, and show up in support of an all-too-big community of gun violence survivors when they need it most.

In February 2021, I became an active member of the Moms Demand Action Massachusetts Community Partnerships team. Together with just a handful of volunteers, I help develop and maintain relationships with community-based organizations whose missions are strategically tied to our work to end gun violence.

My sister Amanda and nephew Gavin (left) with me and my daughter Talia (right) at the Moms Demand Action Massachusetts Wear Orange event in 2019.

If you too want to get involved or are looking for a place to start, here are some fantastic resources:

EVERYTOWN SURVIVOR NETWORK
https://everytownsupportfund.org/everytown-survivor-network/

The Everytown Survivor Network welcomes anyone who has personally experienced gun violence—whether they have witnessed an act of gun violence, been threatened or wounded with a gun, or had someone they know and cared for wounded or killed. This can include but is not limited to gun homicides, gun suicides, domestic violence involving a gun and unintentional shootings.

MOMS DEMAND ACTION FOR GUN SENSE IN AMERICA
https://momsdemandaction.org/

Moms Demand Action is a grassroots movement of Americans fighting for public safety measures that can protect people from gun violence. The group work to pass stronger gun laws and to close the loopholes that jeopardize the safety of our communities.

INSPIRING COMFORT
https://www.inspiringcomfort.com/

Inspiring Comfort, dedicated to cultivating human care and connection, is the pioneer in establishing comfort as a teachable skill. Its mission is to create a culture of comfort in our society.

ORANGE RIBBONS FOR JAIME

https://orangeribbonsforjaime.org/

Following the murder of Jaime Guttenberg at her high school in Parkland, FL., her parents formed Orange Ribbons for Jaime (ORFJ), a 501(c)3 to honor their daughter by supporting causes important to her in life and also causes that deal with the way her life was tragically cut short.

THE GALEN GIBSON FUND

https://goneboy.com/

The Galen Gibson Fund is a state and federally registered non-profit organization. It is privately endowed and continues to be supported by private and public donations. Since its establishment in 1998, the fund has contributed to local educational initiatives, to community and faith-based groups that work with victims of gun violence, and to organizations that promote commonsense gun laws.

BRADY CAMPAIGN TO END GUN VIOLENCE

https://www.bradyunited.org/

Brady's emphasis on education, litigation, and legislation will ensure every community is safe, not only from mass shootings, but from the daily urban gun violence that plagues so many American cities.

DR. KELLY MCGONIGAL, 'HOW TO MAKE STRESS YOUR FRIEND,' TEDGLOBAL 2013

https://www.ted.com/talks/kelly_mcgonigal_how_to_make_stress_your_friend

Psychologist Kelly McGonigal urges us to see stress as a positive and introduces us to an unsung mechanism for stress reduction: reaching out to others.

GIFFORDS

https://giffords.org/

Giffords is a leader in the movement to end gun violence in America. Led by former Congresswoman Gabrielle Giffords, the organization brings decades of political, legal, and policy expertise to the fight for gun safety.

ACKNOWLEDGMENTS

To the beautiful beings who, without hesitation, agreed to share their stories with me, especially those who said yes before I even knew what I was doing: I owe you the world.

Mom, Amanda, Greg, Shannon, Rob, Marci, Eliza, Mike, and Leona—thank you. I couldn't have made this book without you.

To my family, including my partner Drew and my baby girl Talia: Your support day in, day out, late nights in, and late nights up got me here, where I get to see some of my very own dreams come true.

I love you more.

To Professor Eric Koester who jumped on the phone with me when I told him I maybe, sort of, kind of think I might want to explore writing a book someday and said, "Someday is today."

You gave me confidence I didn't know was possible, pushed me to tell more of my own story than anyone else's, and heard me like no stranger ever heard me before. Thank you for believing in me.

To my publisher New Degree Press, editors Katie, Brandy, and Alayna, author coaches, design team, copy editors, and proofreaders—wow.

You are gifting the next generation of authors the tools they need to set themselves up to succeed. I can't wait to see how you grow and to continue our relationship.

And to my author community—YOU. Your outpouring of immediate support inspired me to make this written piece of myself what it is today. Shoutout specifically to my designated beta reader and writing confidant, Eric Beato!

Much like I've experienced throughout my life, you showed me what is possible when you find your people. Thank you for being my people:

Adam Orlando
Aimee Levesque
Alex Mehta
Alexandra Doyle
Alexandra Newsome
Alicia DiPietro
Alison Moppett
Alli Flaherty
Amanda Kartun
Amanda wait
Andrea Reeves
Andrew Zieff
Angela Christiana
Anita Hall
Anthony DiPietro
Ashleigh Phelps
Ashley hoban
Avi Urbas

Barbara DiPietro

Barbara Spies Blair

Brady Plevac

Bryan Lipiner

Cait Kennedy

Caitrin Adelman

Carin Grimes

Carmen Suen

Carolyn Wahid

Cathleen Cahill

Charlene DiPietro

Charlene Foss

Cheryl Milligan

Christine Menard

Cindy Swett

Courtney Rosales

Daniel Ball

Danielle Griggs

David Swett

Donna Coco

Ed and Eileen Maurer

Eliza Valori

Elizabeth Pawlicki

Emilie Gallios

Emily Levy and Yousef Al-Humaidhi

Emily Candib

Emily and Jon Carell

Emily Groccia

Emma Nollman

Eric Beato

Eric Koester

Erin Freda

Francesca Robertson

Gillian Polk

Ian Gale

Ileana Valcarcel

James Kiley

James Regal

Jayna Barry

Jean Conroy

Jen Marr

Jen Orlando

Jennifer Roberts

Jessica Bennett

John Crawford

Jordan Seefeldt

Joseph DiPietro

Julie Thayer and Mike Zerdelian

Kait Lanthier

Karen and Ralph Landry

Karen Dowell

Kathleen McKinnon

Kathy Gill

Katie Warjas

Kelley Michael

Kelli Bennett

Kelsey Happel Olivere

Kelsey Knipstein

Kerry Rourke

Kimberly Henry

Kim Danish

Krista MacKenzie

Kristen Getchell

Kristina Feasey

Laura Beohner
Laura Glass
Lauren Bartleson
Leigh Hope Fountain
Lindsay Magoon
Lindsey Cunningham
Liz Higgins
Lori Glynos
Lyyn Hendrickson
Marci Zieff
Marianne OMera
Marielle Bohan-Baker
Marilyn Robertson
Matt Nollman and Becca Leach
Megan Yeremian
Melissa Jolly
Michael Chmura
Michelle Larcom
Mike Bruny
Mike and Bev Nollman
Mitchell Nollman
Patty Roundy
Phill Gordon
Rachel McInnis
Rebecca Lynch
Samantha Hickie
Sara Zieff
Sarah Francomano
Sarah McGann
Sarah Sykora
Sarah Whitney Humphrey
Shannon Sweeny

Shelley DiPietro Mullarkey
Stacey Lee Coonrad
Stefan Edick
Stephanie Gordon
Susan Gould Coviello
Travis Ziebro
Zundry Padra

APPENDIX

——

INTRODUCTION

American Psychological Association. "Trauma." Accessed June 17, 2021. https://www.apa.org/topics/trauma.

Everytown Research & Policy. "Gun Violence in America." Accessed June 17, 2021. https://everytownresearch.org/report/gun-violence-in-america/.

Langner, Paul. "Attempt at Peace Proved Fatal." *The Boston Globe*, June 19, 1997.

The Center for Treatment of Anxiety and Mood Disorders. "What is Trauma." Accessed June 17, 2021. https://centerforanxiety disorders.com/what-is-trauma/.

CHAPTER 1

Lynch Cantillon Funeral Home. "Jeremy R. 'Jerry' McIntire." Accessed June 17, 2021. https://lynch-cantillon.com/obituaries/2012/11/28/jeremy-r-mcintire/.

CHAPTER 5

Dobrin, Isabel. Garofalo, Michael. "25 Years Later, He Speaks to the Man Who Killed His Son." NPR, December 8, 2017. https://www.npr.org/2017/12/08/568929063/simon-s-rock-shooting-anniversary.

Everytown for Gun Safety. "Our History." Accessed June 17, 2021. https://www.everytown.org/about-everytown/history/.

Everytown Support Fund. "Everytown Survivor Network." Accessed May 4, 2021. https://everytownsupportfund.org/everytown-survivor-network/.

Gibson, Gregory. *Gone Boy: A Father's Search for the Truth in His Son's Murder.* Berkeley, California: North Atlantic Books, 1999.

Greg Gibson. "Meeting the Man Who Killed My Son." May 10, 2019. Video, 4:52. https://www.youtube.com/watch?v=3KZmtAb2ke8.

Ramos, Nestor. "How a Gloucester Author and the Man Who Killed His Son Teamed Up on Gun Reform." *The Boston Globe*, March 25, 2019. https://www.bostonglobe.com/metro/2019/03/25/how-killer-and-gloucester-man-whose-son-killed-teamed-gun-reform/zue1vJv7ClNQZ3wBaMKd3N/story.html.

CHAPTER 6

A Bullseye View (blog). "Target Addresses Firearms in Stores." July 2, 2014. Accessed June 17, 2021. https://corporate.target.com/article/2014/07/target-firearms-policy.

Everytown for Gun Safety. "Target: Create Gun Sense Policies in Your Stores." Accessed June 17, 2021. https://act.everytown.org/sign/target-petition.

Everytown Research & Policy. "Gun Violence in America." Accessed June 17, 2021. https://everytownresearch.org/report/gun-violence-in-america/.

Moms Demand Action. "Moms Demand Action Applauds Target for Asking Customers to Leave Their Guns at Home in Response to Moms' Campaign." Moms Demand Action press release, July 2, 2014. https://momsdemandaction.org/moms-demand-action-applauds-target-asking-customers-leave-guns-home-response-moms-campaign/, accessed June 17, 2021.

Watts, Shannon. *Fight Like A Mother: How a Grassroots Movement Took on the Gun Lobby and Why Women Will Change the World*. San Francisco, California: HarperOne, 2019.

CHAPTER 8

Bado, Kirk. "Bill Toughens Law on Domestic Abusers." Tennessean, June 9, 2016. https://www.tennessean.com/story/news/politics/2016/06/09/bill-toughens-law-domestic-abusers/85642518/.

Brady United. "History of Brady." Accessed June 17, 2021. https://www.bradyunited.org/history.

Kellar, Liz. "Gov. Gavin Newsom OKs Expansion of Laura's Law throughout California." The Union, September 25, 2020. https://www.theunion.com/news/gov-gavin-newsom-oks-expansion-of-lauras-law-throughout-california/.

Kleist, Trina. "10 Years Ago: Right treatment could have averted tragedy, family says." The Union, January 8, 2016. https://www.theunion.com/news/10-years-ago-right-treatment-could-have-averted-tragedy-family-says/.

LaPierre, Wayne. "NRA: Full Statement by Wayne LaPierre in Response to Newtown Shootings." The Guardian. December 21, 2012. https://www.theguardian.com/world/2012/dec/21/nra-full-statement-lapierre-newtown.

Obama, Barack. "Transcript: President Obama at Sandy Hook Prayer Vigil." NPR, December 16, 2012. https://www.npr.org/2012/12/16/167412995/transcript-president-obama-at-sandy-hook-prayer-vigil.

CHAPTER 10

Creating Calm. "Creating Calm." Accessed June 17, 2021. https://creating-calm.com/.

CHAPTER 12

DiPietro, Shelley. "Family of Gunshot Victim has Received Plenty of Support." The Salem Evening News, June 5, 1998.

Facebook, Fred Guttenberg at a Vigil on February 15, 2018: https://www.facebook.com/watch/?v=10156649144186336

Guttenberg, Fred. Find The Helpers: What 9/11 and Parkland Taught Me About Recovery, Purpose, and Hope. Coral Gables, Florida: Mango Publishing, 2020.

Saad, Lydia. "What Percentage of Americans Own Guns?" Gallup, August 14, 2019. https://news.gallup.com/poll/264932/percentage-americans-own-guns.aspx.

Schaeffer, Katherine. "Key Facts About Americans and Guns." Pew Research Center. https://www.pewresearch.org/fact-tank/2021/05/11/key-facts-about-americans-and-guns/.

ENDNOTES

———

1 Name changed

2 Name changed

3 Name changed

4 Name changed